MASTERING THE ART OF IKEBANA

A Guide to Traditional Japanese Flower Arrangement

Kon Osamu

Copyright © 2023 Kon Osamu

All Rights Reserved

No Part of This Book May be Reproduced Without Written Permission By the Author

INTRODUCTION	8
CHAPTER ONE	11
IKEBANA, THE JAPANESE MAGNIFICENCE	11
WHAT IS IKEBANA?	12
A. Origins	15
IKEBANA, JAPANESE CULTURE AND ZEN PHILOSOPHY; THE INTERSECTION	23
ZEN PHILOSOPHY	23
KEY ELEMENTS OF IKEBANA	27
A. LINE(KIREI)	27
B. HARMONY(WA)	28
D. RHYTHM (MIYABI)	31
F. DOMINANCE (SHIN)	34
G. SUBORDINATION(SOE)	35
H. NATURAL FORMS (SHIZEN)	36
I. CULTURAL SIGNIFICANCE	38
K. EMPTINESS(MA)	40
THE MAJOR IKEBANA SCHOOLS	41
1. IKENOBO SCHOOL	42

2. OHARA SCHOOL — 44
4. ICHIYO SCHOOL — 49
5. MISHO SCHOOL — 51
6. RYOBI SCHOOL — 53

CHAPTER TWO — 56
MATERIALS AND TOOLS — 56
   VASES AND CONTAINERS — 59
   SCISSORS AND KNIVES — 60
   ACCESSORIES — 62

CHAPTER THREE — 64
TECHNIQUES AND STYLES/ TYPES — 64
   SHOKA STYLE (FORMAL LINEAR ARRANGEMENTS) — 65
   HEIKA STYLE (STEM-ARRANGED) — 67
   RIKKA STYLE (STANDING FLOWERS) — 70
   NAGEIRE STYLE (THROWN-IN FLOWERS) — 74

CHAPTER 4 — 80
ADVANCED TECHNIQUES IN IKEBANA — 80
   A. Combining Flowers and Foliage — 80
      Embrace Diversity — 80
      Compose with Contrast — 81
      Weaving Foliage as a Tapestry — 81
      Unity in Diversity — 82
      Examples of Flower and Foliage Combinations — 82
   B. Creating Movement and Balance — 85
      Embrace the Flow — 85
      Find Equilibrium — 85
      Capture Movement — 86
      Harmonizing Colors and Textures — 86
      Notable Arrangements that Create Movement and Balance — 87
   C. Using Color and Shape — 89
      The Language of Color — 89
      Examples of Color and Shape Combinations — 89
   The Art of Incorporating Accessories — 91
      Adornments — 91
      Ikebana Accessories that Can Enhance Your Design

- 92
- Seasonal Ikebana — 100
  - Spring Ikebana — 100
  - Spring Ikebana Flower Arrangements to Inspire You — 102
  - Summer Ikebana: Warmth and Vitality — 104
  - Summer Ikebana Flower Arrangements to Inspire You — 105
  - Autumn Ikebana: Embrace the Warmth and Vivid Colors of the Season — 108
  - Autumn Ikebana Flower Arrangements to Inspire You — 109
  - Winter Ikebana: Embracing the Tranquility of the Season — 110
  - Winter Ikebana Flower Arrangements to Inspire You — 111
  - General Seasonal Ikebana Tips: Unleash Your Artistic Magic with Nature's Beauty — 113

Chapter 5 — 116
Creating Your Own Ikebana Arrangements — 116
- Planning and Preparation — 116
  - Create the Right Atmosphere for Your Vision — 116
  - Equip Yourself with the Right Tools — 116
  - Select Flowers and Foliage — 116
  - Prepare Your Workspace — 117
  - Trim and Condition Your Flowers — 117
  - Visualize Your Creation — 117
  - Set the Right Foundation — 117
- Step-by-Step Instructions — 117
  - Step 1: Preparation — 118
  - Step 2: Arrangement — 118
- Troubleshooting Tips — 120
  - Wilting Woes — 120
  - Balancing Act — 121
  - Space Odyssey — 121
  - Structural Snags — 121
  - Colors Collide — 122
  - Learn through Adaptation — 122

- Inspiration and Resources 122
  - Nature's Embrace 122
  - The Poetry of Art 123
  - Cultural Treasures 123
  - Blooming Community 123
  - Ikebana Publications 123
  - Floral Flair 123

Chapter 6 125
THE IMPORTANCE OF IKEBANA 125
- Ikebana Is a Reflection of Harmony and Balance 125
- Ikebana is A Pilgrimage of the Soul 125
- Embracing Minimalism and Simplicity 126
- Ikebana Is An Expression of the Seasons 126
- Ikebana Connects Artists From All Over the World 126
- Ikebana is a Paradigm of Self Discovery 126
- Ikebana Is a Source of Joy and Inspiration 127
- Ikebana Is An Epoch of Legacy and Renewal 127
- Ikebana Cultivates Mindfulness and Connection 127
- Ikebana Is A Timeless and Ever-Evolving Art Form 128
- Ikebana is An Art of Mindful Connection 128
- Ikebana Is A Bridge Between Past and Future 128
- Ikebana Is A Language of Beauty and Expression 129
- Ikebana Embraces Imperfection and Wabi-Sabi 130
- Ikebana Is A Sustainable Art Form 130
- Ikebana Is A Path to Growth 131
- Ikebana Is A Source of Inspiration for Other Art Forms 131
- Ikebana Is An Everlasting Legacy 131

Chapter 7 133
THE ROLE OF IKEBANA IN JAPANESE CULTURE 133
- Ikebana and Japan's Expression of Harmony and Balance 133

- Ikebana As an Emblem of Japan's Cultural Heritage 134
- Ikebana and Japan's Tea Ceremony 135
- Ikebana As a Symbol of Japanese Spiritual Beliefs 136
- Ikebana's Role in Enhancing Interior Spaces in Japanese Culture 137
- Ikebana's Role in Fostering Cultural Identity and Expression 138
- Ikebana and Japan's Appreciation for Nature and Seasons 139
- Ikebana and Its Connection to Japan's Ancestral Roots 139
- Ikebana Embodies Japanese Aesthetics 140

CHAPTER 8: BONUS CHAPTER 141
DIY IKEBANA - MY PERSONAL IKEBANA TIPS TO YOU 141
- MISTAKES AND LESSONS 141
- PRACTICE MAKES PERFECTION 142
- DOs and DON'Ts OF IKEBANA 142
  - Dos of Ikebana 142
  - Don'ts of Ikebana 143
- DIY IKEBANA ARRANGEMENT YOU CAN TRY OUT ON YOUR OWN 144
  - Minimalist Elegance 144
  - Serenity in a Bowl 145
  - Vibrant Verticality 145
  - Nature's Harmony 145
  - Blossoms in the Wind 146

Conclusion 147
Final Thoughts and Next Steps 147

INTRODUCTION

What comes to your mind when you think about the Japanese?

Their tea ceremonies? Their architecture? Samurai and Ninjas? Sumo wrestling? Arcade machines? Kimonos? Godzilla?... and the list goes on and on. Whatever comes to your mind when you think about the Japanese reflects your interests and what aspect of the Japanese you are exposed to. Undoubtedly, the Japanese are known for many things, but one of the aspects of the Japanese context that stands out the most is the art.

Art is an integral aspect of Japanese society and has a rich history dating back thousands of years. Ancient Japanese art is believed to have originated in about 10,000 BCE and includes calligraphy, architecture, paintings, jade carvings, sculpture and pottery. Japanese art has distinctive aesthetics; however, Japanese artists have a history of being influenced by Chinese art and Buddhism, among other influences. It is important also to note that a significant aspect of Japanese art is its typical reflection of the culture's perspective of spirituality and nature. A significant aspect of art within the Japanese context has been influenced by 'Shintoism,' which presents a notion that nature and spirituality are intimately tied together.

Vincent Van Gogh, one of the most prominent influences on the history of Western art, gave the following submission in describing Japanese art:

"If you study Japanese art, you see a man who is undoubtedly wise, philosophic and intelligent, who spends his time how? In studying the distance between the Earth and the Moon? No. In studying the policy of Bismarck? No. He studies a single blade of grass. But this blade of grass leads him to draw every plant and then the seasons, the wide aspect of the countryside, then animals, then the human figure. So, he passes his life, and life is too short to do the whole."

Indeed, Van Gogh's description of Japanese art presents the depth and encompassing nature of the art. Japanese art goes beyond the surface and basic expectation; it is as though each layer of the art leads to further layers which one may not be able to explore completely till they leave the Earth. This is the beauty of Japanese art, as it takes the artist and the admirer of the art on an amazing journey into the limitless depths of the artistic plane.

Artistry has played an essential role in Japanese culture for many centuries. Today, you find many admirers of and participants in Japanese artistic culture, exploring the art, no matter its form. The Japanese government has also greatly encouraged Japanese artistic endeavor. This is done through the support and patronage of institutions such as schools, libraries and museums. An intentional effort has been put into preserving the artistic sphere of the Japanese, with many artistic works being designated as intangible cultural property (mukei bunkazai). Furthermore, specific artists and prominent artistry figures are considered living national treasures (Ningen kokohu).

When it comes to the types and forms of art the Japanese enjoy, there is a wide variety. For instance, European artistic forms such as orchestral and classical music are widely celebrated in the Japanese context. Consequently, various institutions allow people to explore careers in classical music. Traditional Japanese art forms like bunraku (puppet theatre) and noh and kabuki (stylized drama) are widely accepted and enjoyed by many.

Fine art, such as shodo (calligraphy), origami (paper folding), and woodblock printing (ukiyo-e), among others, are strong pillars of Japanese art. There is another very important aspect of Japanese art which includes traditional cultural activities like sado (tea ceremony), bonsai (growing miniature trees), and Ikebana (flower arranging). These art forms are distinctive and often take years of training because of all the work that goes into them. This book shall explore one of these forms of art – Ikebana. However, before we delve into the crux of the artistic concept, it is important to shed light on the significance of art on the Japanese landscape.

Undoubtedly, Japanese art has left a lasting cultural, historical and artistic impression on Japan and the global artistic context. The following are ways that this impression has been presented.

1. **Historical insight:** Japanese artistry is a window into the county's rich history, which dates back to centuries of artistic metamorphosis. Japanese art gives great insight into different eras' political, social and religious spheres. Consequently, historians can grasp the cultural intricacies better and present them to us in a relatable manner.

2. **Cultural identity:** Undoubtedly, Japanese art reflects the nation's distinct cultural identity, values and world perspective. It encapsulates interesting concepts such as the appreciation of imperfection (Wabi-sabi), harmony with nature (Shizen), and the pursuit of simplicity (Kazo). Through various art expressions, the Japanese display their strong connection with the natural world and their respect for customs and traditions.

3. **Spiritual and philosophical profundity:** Many forms of Japanese art, including tea ceremonies, calligraphy, Zen gardens and Ikebana, are closely knitted with spiritual and philosophical practices. These art forms provide a platform for mindfulness, contemplation and meditation, contributing to personal development and inner reflection.

4. **Preservation of customs and traditions:** Japanese artistry plays a pivotal role in sustaining and passing down cultural practices and traditional techniques from generation to generation. Many art expressions, such as traditional theatre and flower arranging (Ikebana), are continually practiced and celebrated to preserve cultural heritage.

5. **Visual and aesthetic appeal:** Japanese art is notable for its excellent craftsmanship, intricacies and emphasis on visual stimulation. The employment of accurate techniques, delicate materials and careful attention to detail result in art that is visually enthralling and emotionally triggering.

Ultimately, the significance of Japanese art is in its ability to encompass history, cultural values and artistry while continually inspiring and captivating people across the globe. Indeed, it mirrors a strong connection between the old and the new age and Japan and the global community.

Having laid a solid foundation on Japanese artistry in general, it is time to shed light on a specific aspect of Japanese art, which has been mentioned a few times. That aspect of Japanese art is Ikebana – the art of "arranging flowers" or, in some other contexts, "giving life to flowers."

Ikebana, a type of Japanese flower arrangement, has existed for a long time, from being used as temple offerings to being a point of attraction in Japanese culture today. It has become an integral part of the Japanese way of life that both experts and novices cherish.

With Ikebana, the Japanese have presented the world with a scientific arrangement of flowers that stand out among others and bring the beauty and refreshment of bringing flowers into our homes.

This book takes a deep dive into the ancient concept of Ikebana and all you need to know about it. It provides great insight to you if you are experienced and interested in flower art. Furthermore, it also serves as an excellent source of great exposure for you if you are getting familiar with the world of flowers and their arrangements. I implore you to lay aside every preconceived notion and be open-minded so you can get all you need from this book. Rest assured that after delving into the amazing world of Ikebana, your perception of life and beauty will change for good.

Now to the million-dollar question – are you ready to journey into a rich aspect of Japanese culture and see flowers "come alive" on the pages of this book?

CHAPTER ONE

IKEBANA, THE JAPANESE MAGNIFICENCE

"Just as musicians express themselves through the language of music, Ikebana artists must use the language of flowers."

-Teshigahara's Diary

WHAT IS IKEBANA?

If I was asked to guess the meaning of Ikebana without prior knowledge of the word. I'd probably call it "a Japanese fighting technique," "a meal," or probably" a position of authority." You might have been thinking the same way the first time you heard the word too

While the word, Ikebana sounds like it would fit into any of the above categories, it has nothing to do with them. In simple terms, Ikebana can be described as the Japanese art of flower arranging that focuses on form and balance. However, this definition only partially captures the word's true meaning in the Japanese context. So, we should examine it in that context.

Ikebana is a term that originates from the combination of 'Hikaru,' a Japanese word which implies 'to arrange, have life, be living,' and 'Hana,' which refers to flowers. The combination of both words can be translated as "giving life to flowers" or "arranging flowers." It is expedient to note that Ikebana transcends putting flowers into a container; it is a disciplined art form in which the arrangement is a living thing. It is that plane where nature and humanity are joined together in beautiful harmony.

While non-Japanese people may perceive Ikebana as simply the art of flower arranging, a more precise translation is "to give life to flowers." Consequently, Ikebana can be thought of as a living floral arrangement. Ikebana is also called 'Kado,' which means "way of flowers."

The Ikebana tradition is deeply rooted in Japan's history, starting with the native belief system of the country – Shinto. Shinto is often regarded as a nature-based religion and typically incorporates practices that center on honoring and celebrating nature, seasons, land and people's relationships with these elements. In Shinto customs, shrines with various elements, including seasonal flower arrangements, were (and still are) constructed in honor of a kami.

Ikebana in the modern day still recognizes the seasons, as many flowers and other Ikebana elements relate to specific holidays and seasons.

Ikebana is not limited to being used to adorn Buddhist alters; its floral arrangements are loaded with rich symbols. Furthermore, creating an Ikebana design is regarded as a spiritual or meditative practice.

Ikebana floral arrangements should typically include design elements or a triangular structure that typifies heaven, Earth and humanity existing in harmony. There are usually three branches of different lengths (Shushi), representing the three symbolic elements of heaven, Earth and humanity. The longest branch is called 'shin,' and it symbolizes heaven. The mid-length branch is called 'soe,' and it is a symbol of humanity. Finally, the shortest branch is called 'hike,' a symbol for the Earth.

The practice of Ikebana can also be regarded as a meditative practice. In Ikebana, an interesting reality is that the journey is equally important as the final destination. The means to the end is just as important as the end.

Sofu Teshigahara, the founder of Sogetsu School, said the following about Ikebana; "Ikebana is not just about sticking a flower into a vase; it is about the love and need of the artist to create beautiful forms…Ikebana is not just about flowers; it is about the person who arranges them."

From Sofu's submission, it is clear that as opposed to the Western habit of casually placing flowers in a vase, Ikebana is more interested in bringing out the inner qualities of flowers and other live materials. Like in sculpture, the concept of realism is prioritized in Ikebana. Elements like line, color, form and function influence the creation of Ikebana. Consequently, the results of merging all these elements are only sometimes predictable; they can range widely in composition and size.

Apart from the fact that flowers, plants and trees in Japanese culture are seasonal, they also come with a lot of symbolism. These factors are very influential in determining the arrangements in Ikebana. Some of the most common elements used in Ikebana include but are not limited to:

    a. Pine and Japanese plum branches around the new year

    b. Narcissus and Japanese iris in the spring

    c. Bamboo grass all through the year

    d. Peach branches for Girls' Day in March

    e. Chrysanthemum in autumn

    f. Cow lily in summer

At times, practitioners of Ikebana trim flowers and branches into unrecognizable shapes; they may even proceed to paint the leaves of an element. Furthermore, plant limbs may be arranged so that they sprout into space. However, balance remains a very major element in all of this.

When it comes to the concept of Ikebana, it is never enough to have beautiful materials at your disposal; these materials must be explored so much that you can create something even more beautiful. One meticulously placed flower can give an effect as powerful as that which is given by an elaborate arrangement.

Both professionals and amateurs can practice the art of Ikebana, and anyone under each category can achieve amazing results; however, like what typically applies in many other art forms, understanding the basics is necessary for success in the practice of the art.

Precision is a core value in Japanese culture, incorporated into the Ikebana curriculum for beginners. They are taught how to properly cut branches and flowers, measure angles in space to place branches and stems correctly, and preserve live materials.

Another vital practice taught in the art of Ikebana is sensitizing eyes to the materials used. This is to the end that practitioners of Ikebana can bring out the inner qualities of materials and understand how these qualities evolve with changes in arrangements.

Essentially, Ikebana is a multidimensional art form that encapsulates the core of Japanese culture, Zen philosophy and a profound celebration of the beauty and impermanence of nature. It attracts individuals to a reflective and artistic practice that cultivates the outer and inner worlds.

HISTORY OF IKEBANA

Having grasped the definition of the concept of Ikebana, the next logical step to take is a step back in time to understand where it all began with Ikebana. This serves as a solid foundation upon which other aspects of this book will develop.

It is no news that the Japanese are notable for their appreciation of beauty and nature, which can be traced to Shinto, Japan's prehistoric native religion. The Japanese have successfully captured nature's beauty into artistic mirrors integrated into daily life. Ikebana is one of Japan's most famous artistic expressions worldwide; it aligns greatly with the Japanese psyche because trees, plants and flowers are great symbols in the Japanese context.

We can trace the beginning of Ikebana to the 6th century when Buddhism arrived on the shores of Japan; it became part of the offerings used to worship Buddha. These offerings were referred to as "huge" and represented a deep sense of reference and spirituality.

For contextual purposes and to properly capture the different stages in its development, the history of Ikebana will be divided into 4 major sections, including origins, development, modernization and global spread.

So, why don't you tighten your seatbelt as we journey back in time to explore the concept of Ikebana?

A. Origins

The author of 'The Art of Arranging Flowers', Shozo Sato, suggests that the origins of Ikebana can be traced back to the 6th century when China presented Buddhism to Japan. Simple flower arrangements (Kuge) were used to reverence Buddha, and this practice developed over time into the more organized art of Ikebana.

The origins of Ikebana can be classified into different categories; these categories include:

    a.   **Religious offerings:** The practice of arranging flowers for religious purposes is rooted in the Japanese indigenous Shinto traditions. Shinto was characterized by offering flowers and other natural elements to spirits as an act of honor and reverence. This laid a foundation for the development of Ikebana.

    b.   **Buddhist influence:** The introduction of Buddhism to Japan from China and Korea in the 6th century caused the evolution of offering flowers for religious purposes. Buddhist monks typically arranged flowers in temple alters and used them to decorate religious spaces. This practice was one that communicated devotion and a harmonious relationship between the spirit realm and the natural world. This integration of floral arrangements into Buddhist practices refined the art of flower arranging and presented new symbolic and aesthetic appeal.

    c.   **Influence of Chinese Culture:** Chinese cultural influences, specifically in flower arrangement and aesthetics, played a major role in influencing the origins of Ikebana. The exchange of artistic ideas, symbolism, and design principles between China and Japan was largely influential in developing Ikebana as a form of art.

China was known for a rich tradition of flower arrangement, which was called "huge" or "keto." This practice entailed the arrangement of flowers in vases to create visually pleasing compositions. It emphasized the use of balance, harmony and symbolism, which eventually became key elements in the Japanese art of Ikebana. The introduction of Zen Buddhism from China to Japan further solidified the exchange of artistic and cultural ideas. Zen philosophy magnified the concepts of mindfulness, simplicity and the appreciation of the present - these concepts were incorporated into Chinese flower arrangements and the Japanese Ikebana.

Undoubtedly, the origins of Ikebana are a blend of cultural influences, religious practices and artistic sensibilities that eventually transformed the basic act of flower arrangement into a more organized and sophisticated form of art.

B. Development

Like the origins, the development of Ikebana finds its bearing in culture, religion and art. After originating from Buddhism, which the Chinese brought to Japanese shores, Ikebana went through different faces of development, which have shaped it into what it has become today. These stages are as follows:

Muromachi period – the emergence of Ikebana (14th-16th century)

The emergence of Ikebana can be traced to the Muromachi period (late 14th century to mid-16th century). In this period, much of what is described as the traditional Japanese art of flower arrangement was developed. The feudal Lords and Generals (Damiyo and Shoguns) gave a group of artists called doboshu the assignment to be in charge of aesthetics and techniques. Some of the doboshu focused on flower arrangement and devised a style involving a standing branch in the center of a vase; this arrangement was called "tatebana" This point marked the beginning of the emergence of masters of flower arrangement. Out of all the masters of flower arrangement that emerged, a monk in the Rokkakudo in Kyoto named Ikenobo Senkei remains the most prominent. His style of tatebana was developed and taught by Ikenobo Senei and Ikenobo Senou and spread through the Samurai class and aristocracy. This style of flower arrangement was accompanied by an increasingly strict form of tea ceremony.

From the Azuchi Momoyama period into the Edo period, Ikebana became a living art form and evolved in major and minor ways.

The following are marks of the development of Ikebana in the Muromachi period:

a. **Integration into cultural practices:** Ikebana got integrated into several aspects of the Japanese culture in this era. Also, it was closely knitted with the tea ceremony (chanoyu), which gained popularity as a common practice that involved hospitality aesthetics and Zen philosophy.

b. **Simplicity and naturalism:** Traditional Japanese arrangements of flowers in the Muromachi era adopted a simpler and more naturalistic approach than earlier extravagant styles. The focus on minimalism and harmony with nature was in sync with the cultural sensibilities of that time, which were clearly influenced by Zen philosophy.

c. **Development of Ikebana styles:** Different styles of Ikebana began emerging in this era, each bringing a distinct approach and principles. The Ikenobo schools, one of the oldest, continued modifying their techniques and arrangements, which contributed to developing Ikebana as an art form.

d. **Zen aesthetics and influence:** The Muromachi period ushered in prosperity in Zen Buddhism, greatly influencing Japanese arts and aesthetics. Ikebana's evolving styles and arrangements mirrored principles like simplicity, mindfulness and emptiness, which find their roots in Zen.

e.   **The rise of the Sogetsu school:** The Sogetsu school is one of the major schools of Ikebana and can be traced back to the Muromachi period. The school's philosophy emphasized creative expression, experimentation and the use of unorthodox materials, departing from the conventional styles.

f.   **Integration of Ikebana in tea ceremony:** Ikebana played a major role in tea ceremony aesthetics in this era. Flowers and arrangements were selected as complements for the seasonal theme and to accentuate the ambience of the tea room.

g.   **Relationship with wabi-sabi aesthetics:** The Muromachi period was also characterized by its emphasis on wabi-sabi aesthetics, which magnifies imperfection and the beauty of simplicity.

h.   **Cultural exchange and Chinese influence:** The Muromachi period experienced a lot of cultural exchange with China and other East Asian countries, which influenced different aspects of Japanese culture, including Ikebana.

The Muromachi period was very pivotal in the development of Ikebana. It is important to note that the influence of Zen philosophy, wabi-sabi aesthetics, and the incorporation of Ikebana into traditional practices like the tea ceremony opened the doors for the continuous evolution of the art form.

Edo period and school diversification (17th – 19th century)

The Edo period came with major shifts in Ikebana art. The samurai class rose in this period, and Ikebana gained popularity among the elite. Furthermore, different Ikebana schools came on board with unique styles and philosophies. Some of these schools include Ikenobo, Enshu, and Ichiyo.

The following are major marks of the evolution of Ikebana in the Edo period:

a. **Samurai and aristocratic patronage:** The Edo period was one in which the Samurai class rose to prominence and held significant cultural and political influence. Ikebana gained popularity among the samurai and aristocracy and became a status symbol in Japanese society.

b. **The emergence of Ikebana schools:** The Edo period was one that featured the introduction and flourishing of Ikebana schools, which came with distinct philosophies, ideologies and aesthetics.

c. **Integration with tea ceremonies and interiors:** In this era, Ikebana formed a solid bond with other traditional art forms—for instance, the Japanese tea ceremony (chanoyu) and interior design.

d. **Seasonal themes and wabi-sabi:** Ikebana arrangements typically integrated seasonal elements and themes during the Edo period. This mirrored the deep connection between nature and Japanese culture. Furthermore, wabi-sabi aesthetics influenced the birthing of Ikebana arrangements that embraced the innate traits of natural materials.

e. **Aesthetics and symbolism:** Ikebana arrangements in the Edo period were known for a deep celebration of nature's beauty and an emphasis on capturing the core of seasonal changes. Furthermore, adopting symbolism played a vital role in Ikebana, with specific flowers chosen to communicate certain meanings and emotions.

f. **Developing styles and techniques:** Different Ikebana schools came on board in the Edo era and introduced unique styles and techniques that mirrored simplicity, asymmetry and the principles of wabi-sabi.

g. **Preservation and evolution:** Ikebana schools in the Edo era emphasized the need to preserve traditional techniques and teachings while adapting to changes in the artistic sphere. Practitioners also continued to look for ways to express their creative juices within the context of established principles.

The Edo era was a time of artistic prosperity for Ikebana. It became an integral element of Japanese culture and mirrored the period's social hierarchies, aesthetic ideals and spiritual intersections. As a result of the era's strong focus on symbolism, seasonal beauty and its incorporation of other art forms, the legacy of Ikebana was greatly strengthened and continues to thrive today.

The Meiji period (1868-1912)

This period marked a major transformation in Japan's history and was characterized by modernization, Westernization and the resurgence of imperial rule. Ikebana experienced major changes as it adapted to the changes in the cultural and societal landscape.

Ikebana evolved in the Meiji period in the following ways:

a. **Western influence and modernization:** The Meiji period was characterized by modernization and Westernization; consequently, the country was open to international trade and ideas. Japanese aesthetics felt the wave of these changes as Western floral arrangement styles and techniques, such as bouquets, started influencing Japanese art.

b. **A shift in aesthetics and techniques:** Due to the influence of Western floral designs, some Ikebana practitioners started integrating foreign flower arrangement techniques into their practice. Ikebana arrangements in this period sometimes featured more colors and vibrant blooms, techniques strange to the typical conservative color palettes of earlier periods.

c. **Impact on traditional art:** Traditional art, including Ikebana, experienced a lot of challenges as they tried to get used to the changes brought about by modernization. Ikebana schools and practitioners struggled to balance preserving ancient techniques and incorporating new ones.

d. **Preservation:** Some practitioners of Ikebana and scholars decided to document traditional Ikebana styles as they recognized the significance of preserving the Japanese cultural heritage.

e. **Ikebana schools:** Existing Ikebana schools, like the Ikenobo school, adapted to the changes in the artistic landscape by modifying their teachings to mirror modern sensibilities while maintaining their core tenets. Notable is that the Sogetsu school, founded in 1927, adopted a more contemporary approach, giving room for greater creative expression and manipulation.

f. **Cultural exchange and interpretation:** The Meiji era also ushered in increased cultural exchange between the Japanese and the West. Consequently, some practitioners of Ikebana began to incorporate elements peculiar to Western art into their arrangements.

g. **Transition to modern Ikebana:** The changes in Ikebana in the Meiji era cleared the path for its evolution in the 20th century. Incorporating modern techniques into traditional Japanese aesthetics opened the door to contemporary Ikebana styles that reflect various artistic expressions.

The Meiji period brought about vital changes in the concept of Ikebana as it struggled with the impact of Westernization and modernization. While traditional principles experienced Western influence, practitioners and schools of Ikebana navigated this period through adaptation, experimentation and finding ways to merge the new and old into an artistic masterpiece.

C. Modernization

Flowing from the Meiji era, the modernization of Ikebana has been a continuous process influenced by various factors, including globalization, cultural shifts and evolving artistic sensibilities.

The modernization of Ikebana can be classified into the following categories:

a. **Late 19th century and Western influence:** As stated earlier, Japan experienced massive modernization in the Meiji era and opened up to Western ideas and practices. Like many other traditional arts, Ikebana faced challenges as the Western influence infiltrated floral designs and arrangements. Consequently, to adapt to the inevitable changes, practitioners of Ikebana began to experiment and incorporate Western techniques into their arrangements.

    b. **20th-century innovation:** The early 20th century brought new Ikebana styles and schools that embraced innovation while preserving the fundamental traditional principles. This period encouraged artistic freedom, creative expression and using unorthodox materials.

    c. **Contemporary experimentation:** Ikebana practitioners of the mid-20th century and beyond began experimenting with new forms, compositions and materials. Consequently, a wider range of creative expressions emerged within the art form. Practitioners began incorporating unusual elements like metal, plastic and other non-traditional elements into their arrangements.

d. **Globalization and cultural exchange:** Ikebana gained international popularity and was presented to audiences worldwide through cultural exchange initiatives and exhibitions. On the other hand, international practitioners of Ikebana presented their cultural perspectives and influences, which led to the amalgamation of Ikebana with various artistic traditions.5

e. **Environmental and sustainability focus:** Typically, modern Ikebana practitioners incorporate themes that communicate environmental sustainability and the preservation of nature in their arrangements. Arrangements also reflect concerns about ecological balance and the interaction between man and the natural world.

f. **Digital media and documentation:** The digital age we are in now gives room for the documentation and distribution of Ikebana arrangements on a global scale. Social media provides a solid platform for practitioners to showcase their works and interact with a wider audience.

g. **Diverse styles and interpretations:** Contemporary Ikebana encapsulates a diverse range of styles, from traditional to avant-garde. Artists typically merge traditional techniques with modern aesthetics, cultural orientations and personal expressions.

h. **Educational accessibility:** Modern technology has brought Ikebana to everyone's fingertips, with online tutorials, workshops and classes designed for a global audience.

Undoubtedly, the modernization of Ikebana encompasses a balance between the preservation of traditional principles and the embrace of innovation. Undeniably, the art form has evolved to accommodate different cultural and artistic influences while maintaining its core tenets of balance, beauty and the intersection between humanity and nature.

D. Global spread

The global spread of the Japanese art of flower arrangement has been an amazing phenomenon that highlights artistic celebration, cultural exchange and the flexibility of traditional practices in a global context.

Below are the paths Ikebana has taken to spread around the world:

a. **Cultural diplomacy and exchange:** International audiences got introduced to Ikebana through cultural exchange programs, exhibitions and diplomatic initiatives. The Japanese government and Ikebana organizations are intentional about spreading the gospel of Ikebana as a means of cultural diplomacy, encouraging interest in and understanding of the concept.

   b. **Japanese diaspora:** With the spread of Japanese communities across the globe, the Japanese take their cultural practices, including Ikebana, wherever they go. Furthermore, Ikebana workshops and classes are focal points for preserving a connection to Japanese heritage and culture.

   c. **Workshops, exhibitions and cultural events:** Workshops, exhibitions and cultural events tailored toward Ikebana showcase the beauty of the art form and its distinctive cultural essence. These events attract a wide range of audiences and contribute to the art form's popularity.

d. **Educational resources and online platforms:** The digital age has greatly influenced the spread of Ikebana via online tutorials, instructional videos and classes. Furthermore, social media platforms allow Ikebana enthusiasts to connect and share their works and ideas.

e. **Integration with local culture:** As Ikebana spreads to various regions, it typically blends with local cultural practices, which results in unique interpretations and styles. Local flowers are usually incorporated, blending Japanese tradition and local identity.

f. **Recognition and appreciation:** Ikebana strongly focuses on nature, mindfulness and aesthetics, which many people from various cultural orientations can relate to; consequently, the art form possesses a worldwide appeal. Furthermore, the emphasis of the art form on balance, harmony and artistic expression is not limited by any language barrier.

g. **Ikebana associations and networks:** Global Ikebana networks and associations provide a platform through which practitioners of Ikebana can connect, work together and share their love for the art.

The spread of Ikebana globally reflects its consistent beauty, cultural essence and adaptability. With its spread across borders and cultures, Ikebana has greatly influenced the artistic and creative sphere of various countries as it continuously honors its Japanese origins.

IKEBANA, JAPANESE CULTURE AND ZEN PHILOSOPHY; THE INTERSECTION

Another aspect of shedding light on Ikebana is exploring how it relates to Zen philosophy. Zen philosophy originated in China; since China was a major influence in introducing Ikebana to Japan, it makes sense that it was also introduced to the Japanese.

There is an intersection between Ikebana, Japanese culture and Zen philosophy, a rich and emphatic convergence that highlights the harmony between art, spirituality and cultural expression. This point of intersection is where each component's distinct principles, aesthetics and values merge to birth a unique and contemplative art form.

Since some light has been shed on Ikebana and Japanese culture, the concept of Zen philosophy will be explained, after which we will delve into the intersection between all three.

ZEN PHILOSOPHY

Zen philosophy is a school of Mahayana Buddhism that originated in China and eventually spread to Japan. After it spread to Japan, Zen philosophy greatly influenced various aspects of Japanese culture, including Japanese art, literature, aesthetics and the general way of life. At the core of Zen philosophy is an emphasis on mindfulness, direct experience and the discovery of one's true nature. Zen is known as 'chan' in China and was received with a lot of enthusiasm when it arrived at the shores of China. The Samurai class, who wielded political power at that time, also welcomed Zen, and before long, it became the most prominent form of Buddhism.

The key element of Zen Buddhism is found in its name, as 'zen' means meditation. It teaches that enlightenment is attained through the keen realization that one is already enlightened. This realization can happen gradually or in a flash (this is an emphasis of Soto and Rinzai schools, respectively). This awakening is not automatic and is usually a result of one's effort; deities and scriptures can only offer limited help.

Zen Buddhism strongly emphasizes simplicity and the importance of the natural world and generates a unique aesthetic which is expressed in terms of wabi-sabi. These two concepts are used to communicate a sense of melancholy, rusticity, naturalness, loneliness and age, such that a worn-out, unattractive peasant's jar is considered more beautiful than a carefully crafted exquisite dish. While the carefully crafted dish pleases the senses, the peasant's jar stimulates the mind and emotions such that one can contemplate the essence of reality.

The key concepts of Zen philosophy include:

1. **Direct experience (Kensho/Satori):** Zen emphasizes direct experiential understanding over theoretical knowledge. Kensho or Satori can be described as the instant, intuitive insight into one's true nature or the nature of reality. Zen places a premium on a practical, experiential awakening rather than head knowledge.

2. **Mindfulness and presence:** Practicing mindfulness and being fully present in the present moment are core principles of Zen philosophy. This involves paying attention to daily tasks and experiences, leading to increased awareness and insight.

3. **Non-dualism:** Zen emphasizes the non-dual nature of reality, where differentiation between subject and object, self and other, dematerializes. The concept of non-dualism challenges traditional dualistic thinking and supports a more holistic perspective.

4. **Daily enlightenment:** Zen philosophy is big on the fact that enlightenment is not separate from daily life. There is an intersection between the mundane and the transcendent, and a person can experience moments of awakening or insight in basic actions or interactions.

5. **Emptiness (Sunyata):** Emptiness is a core concept in Zen

and Buddhism. It refers to the idea that all phenomena lack innate, fixed existence. The embrace of emptiness gives room for more flexibility and open-mindedness toward reality.

6. **Impermanence and transience:** Zen esteems the impermanence and temporary nature of all things. Understanding this reality of life leads to a deeper appreciation of each moment.

7. **Koans:** Koans can be defined as paradoxical statements, questions or stories used in Zen to cause deep contemplation and insight. Meditating on Koans fosters a shift in perspective beyond the realms of logic.

8. **Non-attachment:** Zen teaches non-attachment to desires and outcomes, which helps reduce suffering because a person has learned to accept and let go.

9. **Wabi-Sabi aesthetics:** Zen's celebration of imperfection, asymmetry and the beauty of the natural world contributed to the emergence of wabi-sabi aesthetics in Japan. This concept lays an emphasis on the beauty of simplicity, decay, and the authentic.

10. **Master-Student relationship:** Zen typically entails a close relationship between a teacher (roshi) and a student (disciple). Usually, in this relationship, guidance and insight are transformed through personal interaction and experience.

Indeed, Zen philosophy's focus on direct experience, mindfulness and incorporating spiritual practice into everyday life has significantly influenced many aspects of Japanese culture. Furthermore, the philosophy has attracted interest and enthusiasm from people worldwide who seek a deeper understanding of existence and inner peace.

You may have noticed some key concepts in Zen philosophy,

which you also found under the sections about Japanese culture and Ikebana. If you didn't, this is another opportunity to see the intersection between the Japanese culture, Ikebana and Zen philosophy.

Below are some of the key aspects of this intersection:

a. **Simplicity and elegance:** Japanese culture, Ikebana and Zen philosophy all prefer simplicity, minimalism and elegance. Ikebana's adoption of controlled elements and clean lines mirrors this shared ideology.

   b. **Balance and harmony:** Ikebana's emphasis on balance and harmony reverberates the Zen principle of interconnectedness and the essence of achieving equilibrium in every sphere of life.

   c. **Environmental awareness:** Ikebana's celebration of the environment, seasons and the natural world intersect with Japanese practices and Zen's focus on our interconnection with nature.

   d. **Nature's harmony and transience:** Ikebana and the Japanese culture celebrate the beauty of temporariness, mirroring seasonal changes and the fickle nature of life. Furthermore, Ikebana arrangements capture the harmony between man and nature, encapsulating the traditional Japanese honor for the natural world.

   e. **Wabi-Sabi aesthetics:** Celebrating the beauty of imperfection and transience is central to the concept of Ikebana. It mirrors both Japanese cultural tenets and Zen's wabi-sabi aesthetics.

   f. **Mindfulness and the present moment:** The creation of Ikebana requires focused attention and mindfulness, agreeing with Zen's emphasis on being fully present in every situation. The meditative process of flower arrangement provides an opportunity to develop awareness and experience the moment completely.

g. **Spiritual reflection:** Zen philosophy and Ikebana communicate spiritual reflection and self-exploration. Arranging flowers can serve as a form of meditation and a way to connect with the inner self.

h. **Cultural symbolism and tradition:** Ikebana typically incorporates cultural symbols and traditional elements, core aspects of Japanese culture. This connection reiterates the fusion between Ikebana and its cultural context.

i. **Non-attachment and letting go:** Ikebana's temporary arrangement reflects Zen's teaching of non-attachment and the temporariness of things. Creating an arrangement and letting it go reflects Zen's emphasis on non-attachment.

The intersection between Japanese culture, the traditional art of flower arrangement and Zen philosophy births a perfect blend of values, aesthetics and practices. It presents a reflective space for artistic exploration, personal expression and spiritual connection. Consequently, individuals can experience a deeper sense of beauty, presence and meaning.

KEY ELEMENTS OF IKEBANA

It has been established that Ikebana has to do with the arrangement of flowers; however, it goes beyond the mere arrangement of flowers in a vase. The art of Ikebana has a major emphasis on harmony, balance and minimalism. The art seeks to create a deeper connection with nature and the environment.

There are key elements that govern the art of Ikebana, and understanding these elements goes a long way in determining how successful an attempt at Ikebana is.

The key elements of Ikebana include:

A. LINE(KIREI)

Line, a key element of Ikebana, is very fundamental to the intricacies of the traditional art of flower arrangement. The line can be described as the intentional and vital use of strokes and angles in the arranging process to create a distinctive sense of movement, rhythm and visual flow. The line element is crucial in shaping the overall composition and communication of a range of emotions and concepts.

What does the element of line express in Ikebana?

Line in Ikebana expresses the following significant traits:

a.   **Movement:** Practitioners of Ikebana utilize lines to communicate movement and direction in an arrangement. The lines can come in various forms; vertical or horizontal, straight or curved, diagonal or serpentine. An artist skillfully arranging plant materials across these lines typically represents visual movement. This helps to guide the viewer's eye through the arrangement.

> b. **Form:** Lines are also used to express the form and structure of individual components, be it a flower, branch, or leaf. By placing materials along specific lines with precision, an artist is enabled to the distinct shapes, contours and textures of the elements of the plant.
>
> c. **Symbolism:** Symbolism is another significant trait the element of line expresses in the traditional art of arranging flowers. For instance, a straight (upright) line may communicate strength and stamina, while an elegantly curved line may communicate a sense of gentle fluidity. Practitioners of Ikebana may choose lines and

angles to communicate emotions or concepts they desire to project.

d. **Balance:** Lines in Ikebana are also instrumental in bringing a harmonious balance between the various elements of the arrangement. An Ikebana design that qualifies as well-balanced uses lines to share visual weight and create symmetry, ensuring that the arrangement showcases stability and is pleasing to the eye.

e. **Rhythm:** Typically, Ikebana arrangements infuse rhythm by repeating or through the variation of lines. Rhythmically placing plant materials communicates the concept of movement, which captivates the viewer's eye and suggests a feeling of continuity.

f. **Interaction with space:** A pivotal factor in Ikebana is the interaction between the lines of the arrangement and the surrounding space. The meticulous use of negative space surrounding the lines magnifies the overall composition and emphasizes the plant materials' beauty and the emptiness surrounding them.

Undoubtedly, the line element in the traditional art of giving life to flowers is a versatile tool that helps artists incorporate balance, movement and aesthetic appeal into their arrangements. Skillful manipulation of lines by Ikebana by practitioners of Ikebana births arrangements that occupy the senses, compel emotions and showcase an undeniable connection between nature and artistic expression.

B. HARMONY(WA)

Harmony is a fundamental element in the traditional Japanese art of flower arrangement. This element transcends basic visual appeal and creates a sense of unity, balance and correspondence between the various elements in an arrangement. Harmony in Ikebana aims to create a solid relationship between the natural materials, the container and the surrounding space.

Harmony in Ikebana is expressed in the following forms:

a. **Balance and unity:** Harmony in Ikebana is birthed through carefully selecting and arranging plant materials to create a unified and balanced composition. The elements are complementary and support each other to form an organized whole. Unity always contributes to the overall harmonious appearance of an arrangement.

b. **Contrast and complement:** Harmony in Ikebana encapsulates both contrast and complementarity. Contrasting elements like textures and colours can create visual appeal and some degree of dynamic tension. On the other hand, complementary elements accentuate each other's beauty.

c. **Interaction with nature:** A major aim of the traditional flower arrangement is to create a harmonious interaction between the natural world and human creativity. One major way of achieving this is to use plant materials that mirror the changing seasons and integrate them into the arrangement. Ikebana practitioners are known for celebrating the beauty and cycles of nature.

d. **Container selection:** The choice of container plays a role in Ikebana as it interacts with the plant materials to create a sense of harmony. The container's shape, colour and texture must harmonize with the elements, ultimately enhancing the aesthetic appeal. The relationship between the materials and the container should feel integrated and mutually beneficial.

e. **Cultural Significance and Symbolism:** Ikebana often incorporates symbolic elements that enhance the feeling of harmony. The selection and arrangement of plant materials can convey specific meanings or emotions, adding depth to the composition.

f. **Integration with Surroundings:** Harmony in Ikebana extends beyond the arrangement itself and encompasses its relationship with the surrounding space. Whether displayed in a room, a tokonoma (an alcove in architecture), or an outdoor setting, it is important for the arrangement to harmonize with its environment. The negative space around the arrangement ("Ma") is equally significant, creating a sense of harmony.

g. **Personal Expression:** While Ikebana has established principles of harmony, each artist's interpretation and personal style play a role in creating a sense of harmony. Artists can infuse their perspectives and emotions into their arrangements resulting in individual expressions of harmony.

h. **Simplicity and Elegance:** Achieving harmony often involves embracing simplicity and elegance as guiding principles. Ikebana promotes the idea of eliminating elements to emphasize the beauty of the selected materials. This focus on simplicity enhances a feeling of calmness and peacefulness.

Harmony in Ikebana is about creating a great relationship between the various elements, including the container, natural materials, space, and cultural context. Ikebana practitioners typically desire to get a sense of unity, balance and aesthetic organization through careful consideration and well-organized arrangement.

C. BALANCE

Balance is another integral element in the art of Ikebana. Creating harmonious evenness among the various elements in an arrangement brings balance. These various elements include the container, plant materials, space and form. It is important to note that balance is not just about visual parity; it encapsulates the distribution of proportions, visual weight and the encompassing sense of harmony and stability.

Balance is expressed in Ikebana in the following ways:

a. **Asymmetry:** Typically, in Western art, balance embraces symmetry; however, Ikebana usually embraces asymmetry. Asymmetrical arrangements contribute more dynamism and visual stimulation. Ikebana practitioners achieve topnotch equilibrium by meticulously placing elements of various shapes, sizes and colors.

b. **Interaction with space:** In Ikebana, balance extends to the interaction between the arrangement and its surroundings. It is important to note that negative space is as integral as the occupied space and adds to the overall balance and harmony of the arrangement.

c. **Restraint:** Balance in Ikebana typically entails restraint and simplicity. By using a controlled number of elements and sustaining a sense of emptiness, Ikebana practitioners accentuate the beauty of each component and create a balanced composition.

d. **Focal point:** Ikebana arrangements usually showcase a major focal point that attracts attention. On the other hand, the other elements, which are subordinate to the focal point, cooperate to support and bring balance to the arrangement. This intersection between dominance and subordination contributes to balance as an integral element of Ikebana.

e. **Cultural and seasonal context:** Getting balance may involve considering cultural symbolism and changing seasons. Some arrangements are designed to more distinct themes, emotions or seasonal changes. This is a contribution to a balanced reflection of nature and culture.

f. **Contrast and complement:** A practitioner can achieve balance through the contrast and complementarity of different elements. Contrasting colors, textures, shapes and sizes can birth a visually captivating balance that captures the viewer's eye.

g. **Spatial awareness:** Practitioners of Ikebana possess an enhanced awareness of spatial relationships. They meticulously consider the directions and angles of each element to ensure balance and rhythm. This brings about harmony in the arrangement from multiple viewpoints.

h. **Personal expression:** While Ikebana has basic established principles, practitioners have the freedom to bring their uniqueness and creativity to their arrangements. Personal style and interpretation are pivotal in getting a balanced composition.

Balance entails carefully considering placement, proportions and spatial interactions to create an exquisite and emotionally evocative composition that champions the beauty of nature and the art of arrangement.

D. RHYTHM (MIYABI)

Rhythm can be described as a dynamic and subtle element of Ikebana. It refers to the visual flow and progression created by placing elements within the arrangement. Rhythm is a tool through which a practitioner guides the viewer's eye through the arrangement intentionally and engagingly. Rhythm brings a sense of harmony and continuity and adds vitality and energy to the arrangement.

How is rhythm expressed in Ikebana?

Rhythm is expressed in Ikebana in the following ways:

a. **Flow and movement:** Typically, Ikebana practitioners

calculatedly position plant materials to create a sense of progression and flow within the arrangement. This progression can be gotten through the lines, angles and spacing within the arrangement. As a result, the viewer is compelled to follow a natural progression as their eyes move from one element to another.

- b. **Visual Progression:** Rhythm in Ikebana promotes a sense of visual progression. The placement of elements spurs the viewer to look at the arrangement from different angles, unveiling new perspectives and details with every glance.

- c. **Focal points and progression:** Typically, Ikebana includes focal points such as a dominant flower or element to anchor the arrangement. Consequently, the arrangement guides the viewer's eye from the focal point to other elements. This creates a rhythm that guides the gaze along an intentional path.

- d. **Placement and direction:** The elements of a Japanese flower arrangement are typically placed to establish a rhythm. The angles, lines and directions guide the viewer's gaze and create a visual path that adds depth to the composition.

- e. **Contrast and repetition:** Rhythm can also be achieved through calculated contrast and repetition. Contrasting elements like different colours or textures create lively tension and points of interest. Repeating textures, shapes, patterns, or forms strengthens the rhythmic flow of an arrangement.

- f. **Seasonal and cultural influences:** Rhythm in Ikebana can be influenced by seasons and cultural context changes. Usually, seasonal elements are integrated into the arrangement to strengthen its rhythmic flow and bring nature's cyclical rhythm to perspective.

g. **Interaction with space:** The rhythm formed within the arrangement relates to the surrounding empty space. The interaction between occupied and empty spaces contributes to the rhythm and emphasizes the arrangement's visual progression.

h. **Personal expression:** Although certain principles guide Ikebana, the uniqueness of each practitioner is allowed to contribute to the rhythmic flow of the arrangement. Personal expression is pivotal to how rhythm is achieved and the distinctiveness of each Ikebana design.

Like with music, rhythm in Ikebana creates a sense of movement and progression within the arrangement. It captures the viewer's eye and guides their exploration while triggering emotions by intentionally placing certain elements.

E. SIMPLICITY

In Ikebana, simplicity is a foundational and core element. It emphasizes the beauty of restraint and minimalism and focuses on plant materials' important qualities and arrangement. Simplicity is a concept in Ikebana that entails deliberately removing unnecessary elements and birthing a composition emphasizing the elegance of the important components.

Simplicity is expressed in Ikebana in the following ways:

a. **Minimalism:** Ikebana fosters a minimalist approach, in which arrangements are created with a controlled number of elements. By trimming down an arrangement to its core components, a practitioner emphasizes the beauty and purity of each plant material.

b. **Natural beauty:** Simplicity showcases the natural beauty of each plant material. The traditional Japanese flower arrangement seeks to encapsulate the essence of nature rather than relying on extravagant ornamentation.

c. **Cultural and philosophical values:** Simplicity in Ikebana mirrors Japan's wider cultural and philosophical values—for instance, the appreciation of impermanence (wabi-sabi) and the importance of finding beauty daily.

d. **Restricted color palette:** Simplicity typically implies a restrained and harmonious color palette. Ikebana arrangements may adopt a restricted range of colors to evoke a sense of calmness and cohesion.

e. **Personal expression:** Simplicity does not necessarily mean uniformity. Ikebana practitioners can bring their creative juices and interpret their arrangements however they deem fit. They are allowed to introduce their distinctive expressions of simplicity.

f. **Restraint:** Simplicity in the traditional Japanese arrangement of flowers entails a sense of understatement and restraint. The practitioner usually exercises care in positioning each element, birthing an elegant composition.

g. **Focal point:** While Ikebana emphasizes simplicity, a practitioner may still incorporate a dominant element (which serves as a focal point for the arrangement). The focal point draws attention and gives the viewer visual access to the arrangement.

h. **Negative space:** Negative space can also be described as the empty space around and within the arrangement and is a vital part of simplicity in Ikebana. The balance between the occupied and empty spaces contributes to the aesthetic appeal of the arrangement.

i. **Essential forms:** Simplicity in Ikebana entails showing plant materials' inherent lines, shapes and textures. The form of every element is celebrated, and attention is paid to their distinct characteristics.

Simplicity is a guiding principle in Ikebana that emphasizes the minimalism and contemplative nature of the art. With a focus on the vital qualities of plant materials and highlighting their natural beauty, simplicity gives room for deeper interaction with nature.

F. DOMINANCE (SHIN)

Dominance in Ikebana refers to the deliberate emphasis on a focal point or major element within an arrangement. The element of dominance creates a point of focus and sets the tone for the composition from that point, while other elements support and contribute to the dominance of the chosen feature.

Dominance in Ikebana is expressed in the following ways:

a. **Focal point:** Dominance entails choosing a focal point known as the "shin," which is set apart to capture the viewer's eye and become the arrangement's core.

- b. **Hierarchy of elements:** The introduction of the concept of dominance in an arrangement suggests a hierarchy among the various components of that arrangement. Other elements are known as "soe" or subordinate elements and work harmoniously with the dominant element to create a balanced composition.

- c. **Guiding the viewer's eye:** Dominance plays a major role in guiding the viewer's eye through the arrangement. The dominant element serves as a compass which leads the viewer's eye on a journey through the other elements of the composition.

- d. **Visual weight:** Usually, the dominant element carries more visual weight and significance than other elements in the arrangement. The dominant element's placement, size, color and shape make it stand out among other elements and communicate its importance.

e. **Contrast and balance:** In Ikebana, the contrast between the dominant and subordinate elements contributes to the overall balance of the arrangement. The visual weight of the arrangement is distributed in a manner that communicates equilibrium.

f. **Emotional and symbolic significance;** The dominant element in Ikebana often comes with some emotional or symbolic significance. It may represent a season, theme or cultural concept, contributing to the depth and meaning of the arrangement.

g. **Asymmetry and balance:** Dominance comes on board with asymmetry, a common concept in Ikebana. The position of the dominant element can contribute to the overall balance of the arrangement.

h. **Interaction with space:** The position of the dominant element within the arrangement influences the interaction between the arrangement and its surroundings. There is an interaction between negative space and the dominant element, which creates an amazing visual interplay.

i. **Creative expression:** Undoubtedly, dominance is a key principle in Ikebana; however, practitioners can express this principle with their uniqueness. Personal creativity and individual dynamism contribute to the diversity of Ikebana.

Dominance is the emphasis on a focal point in an arrangement which serves as a compass for the viewer's attention and sets the tone for the arrangement.

G. SUBORDINATION(SOE)

Subordination is the opposite of dominance in Ikebana; it is the arrangement of elements to support and emphasize a focal point in an arrangement. Subordination fosters harmony, balance and visual engagement.

It is expressed in Ikebana in the following ways:

a. **Supporting the focal point:** The focal point in an arrangement is the main element that draws attention. Subordination entails placing other elements around the focal point to accentuate its features.

b. **Guiding the viewer's eye:** Subordination is a compass guiding the viewer's gaze through the arrangement. The arrangement's lines and angles, birthed by the positioning of subordinate elements, guide the viewer's eye to the focal point and create a visual path.

c. **Visual hierarchy:** Subordination forms a hierarchy of elements across different levels of an arrangement. While the dominant element takes the spotlight, the subordinate elements cooperate to create a balanced arrangement.

d. **Negative space interaction:** Subordinate elements relate to the negative space in Ikebana. How subordinate elements are positioned with the focal point and surrounding emptiness adds to the balance of the arrangement.

e. **Cultural and seasonal context:** Subordination can also be influenced by cultural symbolism and seasonal change. The choice of subordinate elements may depend on their cultural essence or availability during different seasons.

f. **Balance and harmony:** Subordination adds to the overall balance of the arrangement. The visual weight of the arrangement is shared in a way that communicates a sense of unity.

g. **Personal interpretation:** Practitioners can express and interpret subordination in ways that communicate their uniqueness. This personal touch ensures that every Ikebana arrangement mirrors the practitioner's style.

h. **Contrast and complement:** Subordinate elements can contrast with the dominant element regarding shapes, size, color or texture. The contrast adds some visual appeal and elegant tension to the composition. Concurrently, the subordinate elements should complement the dominant element and accentuate its beauty.

Subordination in Ikebana is about creating an intersection that communicates the harmony between the dominant and subordinate elements within an arrangement. Ikebana artists can create a sense of unity, balance and visual appeal by carefully positioning and arranging elements with the focal point.

H. NATURAL FORMS (SHIZEN)

Ikebana recognizes the inherent beauty of plant materials and aims to emphasize their textures, natural shapes and colors. Natural forms in Ikebana are an element that focuses on the intersection between the natural world and the arrangement and allows viewers to appreciate the organic qualities of the materials.

The element of natural forms is expressed in the following ways:

a. **Focus on authenticity:** Practitioners of Ikebana aim to show plant materials in their true and unaltered state, emphasizing their original forms. This approach is a reflection of respect for the integrity of nature and its intrinsic beauty.

b. **Integration of imperfection:** The traditional Japanese art of flower arrangement embraces the concept of wabi-sabi, which emphasizes beauty in imperfection. Natural forms may include asymmetry, variations and irregularities that add to the authenticity of the arrangement.

c. **Minimal manipulation:** Ikebana is big on minimal manipulation of plant materials. Instead of forcing materials into unnatural shapes, Ikebana practitioners work with natural lines and curves of the materials and create an organic arrangement that reflects harmony.

d. **Cultural significance:** Natural forms in Ikebana may hold some symbolic and cultural meaning. Some specific Japanese flowers or plants may carry some cultural significance or hold certain connotations, adding to the arrangement's depth.

e. **Respect for materials:** Natural forms in Ikebana show respect for the individual characteristics of each plant element. It could be the elegant curve of a branch, the flower's tender petals, or the leaf's texture. All these features are recognized and incorporated into the arrangement.

f. **Interaction with space:** Natural forms relate to the surrounding space in Ikebana. The arrangement's shapes, lines and textures birth a visual communication between the materials and the emptiness around them.

g. **Sync with nature:** Ikebana arrangements typically mirror the changes in seasons and recognize the cycles of nature. Ikebana captures the essence of the natural world by choosing plant materials that characterize a particular season.

h. **Personal expression:** Practitioners have the liberty to bring their personal interpretations and creative juices to the arrangement. Each artist's point of view and artistic voice significantly influence how natural forms are incorporated into the composition.

The element of natural forms in Ikebana highlights the recognition of nature's beauty and authenticity. Ikebana practitioners work with the innate qualities of plant materials and allow their natural forms to shine while also creating visually striking arrangements deeply engrained in the natural world.

I. CULTURAL SIGNIFICANCE

Usually, Ikebana arrangements mirror the cultural context and seasonal changes, saturating the compositions with deeper meanings, symbols and a sense of interaction with nature and the passage of time.

Cultural significance in Ikebana is expressed in the following ways:

> a. **Symbolism:** Some flowers and plants carry specific meanings in Japanese culture. Practitioners of Ikebana may use these materials to communicate concepts, emotions or cultural ideas through their arrangements. For instance, cherry blossoms are typically used to communicate temporariness and the fleeting nature of life.
>
> b. **Awareness of time:** The significance of culture and seasons in Ikebana encourages knowledge of the passage of time and the cyclical nature of seasons. Arrangements emphasize a specific moment to appreciate nature's volatile beauty.
>
> c. Seasonal themes: Ikebana arrangements are usually created to mirror seasonal changes. Various flowers and plant materials are chosen based on natural availability during specific times of the year. This practice communicates the uniqueness and beauty of seasons.

d. **Occasions and celebrations:** The traditional Japanese art of flower arrangement can be used to capture specific ceremonies, occasions or celebrations. The style of arrangement or choice of materials can be influenced by the uniqueness of an event, infusing cultural and symbolic meaning into the composition.

e. **Cultural traditions:** Ikebana typically integrates elements of Japanese cultural traditions. Cultural customs and traditions may influence the arrangement's form, container type, and overall outlook.

f. **Contemplative connection:** Ikebana's cultural and seasonal essence moves viewers to pause and ponder on the beauty and meaning of the arrangement. It generates a contemplative interaction with the natural world and the cultural values it personifies.

g. **Harmony with nature:** Syncing Ikebana with the seasons encourages a sense of harmony with the natural world. Choosing plant materials in season helps birth a composition that reflects the viewer's experience of the environment.

Ikebana's cultural and seasonal essence adds meaning and depth to the art form. Ikebana arrangements become visually appealing and emotionally reflective by incorporating elements of Japanese culture and seasonal changes. This fosters a solid connection with nature, tradition and human experience.

J. ASYMMETRY (FUKINSEI)

While Western floral design typically focuses on symmetry, Ikebana emphasizes asymmetry to create dynamic and visually appealing compositions. This element brings natural beauty, movement and imperfection as it aligns with the principles of wabi-sabi, which recognizes beauty in imperfection and temporariness.

Asymmetry is expressed in the following ways:

a. **Natural beauty:** Asymmetry mirrors the organic contortions found in nature. Practitioners of Ikebana work with the innate shapes and lines of plant materials and allow them to influence the form of the composition.

b. **Movement and flow:** Asymmetrical arrangements usually communicate a sense of progression and flow. The composition's lines and angles guide the viewer's gaze and create an intriguing visual journey.

c. **Negative space:** Asymmetry plays a major role in the interaction of the arrangement with negative space. The empty spaces surrounding the asymmetrical elements add to the harmony and balance of the composition.

d. **Visual interest:** Asymmetry incorporates visual interest and complexity into the arrangement. Unexpected arrangements of elements capture the viewer's eye, compelling viewers to explore the composition from different perspectives.

e. **Embracing imperfection:** Ikebana attaches importance to imperfection and celebrates the volatile nature of existence. Asymmetry gives room for elements to be placed in an unorthodox fashion, acknowledging that perfection can sprout from the imperfect.

f. **Cultural philosophy:** Asymmetry in Ikebana agrees with wider Japanese cultural philosophies, such as wabi-sabi and celebrating impermanence and genuineness.

g. **Dynamic balance:** Asymmetrical arrangements get balance through the detailed placement of various elements, even if they do not reflect on both sides of the arrangement. The visual weight of the arrangement is shared unevenly to birth a harmonious balance.

Asymmetry is an integral part of Ikebana, making it stand out among other floral art forms. Ikebana practitioners can integrate a sense of vitality, organic beauty, and movement into their arrangements by embracing the natural irregularities of plan materials.

K. EMPTINESS(MA)

Emptiness is also known as "ma" and is an integral part of Ikebana. It refers to the concept of space or voidness between and around an arrangement's elements. It is important to note that in Ikebana, the contemplative incorporation of emptiness is as important as the placement of the plant materials. Emptiness contributes to the composition's total rhythm, balance and harmony, accentuating the arrangement's beauty and depth.

Emptiness in the traditional Japanese art of flower arrangement is expressed in the following ways:

a.   **Negative space:** As already stated, the negative space is the area that surrounds and relates to the arranged elements. Practitioners of Ikebana use this space to shape the composition and create a sense of balance and proportion.

    b. **Creating movement:** Emptiness adds to the progression and rhythm of the arrangement. The viewer's perspective is guided through the arrangement as it follows the angles and lines of elements and the emptiness around.

    c. **Symbolism and interpretation:** Emptiness as a concept in Ikebana can have symbolic interpretations and bring about emotions. How emptiness is employed can contribute to the overall theme of the arrangement.

    d. **Enhancing form:** Emptiness magnifies the forms and shapes of the plant materials. The divergence between occupied and empty spaces draws attention to the elegance and distinctiveness of each element.

e. **Multiple perspectives:** Emptiness invites viewers to interact with the arrangement from different perspectives. The intersection between occupied and empty spaces showcases different viewpoints and experiences.

f. **Interaction with elements:** Emptiness interacts with the arranged elements, creating a sense of relationship and interaction. The spaces between elements can communicate a sense of balance, harmony or tension.

g. **Cultural and philosophical significance:** Emptiness is deeply engrained in Japanese aesthetics and philosophy. It mirrors concepts like wabi-sabi and the celebration of simplicity and subtle elegance.

Emptiness is a contemplative element of Ikebana that transcends mere absence. It is a meaningful element that adds depth and a sense of interaction with the arrangement. Ikebana practitioners can create compositions that catch the viewer's eye by skillfully incorporating emptiness with plant materials.

The key elements of Ikebana are those pillars without which an arrangement cannot be successful. These key elements must be adhered to and incorporated religiously to achieve a successful arrangement. Every practitioner or intending practitioner of Ikebana needs an understanding of these key elements of Ikebana.

THE MAJOR IKEBANA SCHOOLS

It will interest you that there are 3,000 – 4,000 Ikebana schools in Japan, each with a unique style run by a different iemoto (a grand master or head of a school). This shows how much the art form has greatly developed over centuries. However, the traditional Japanese art of flower arrangement has major schools that have contributed to its development and spread worldwide. Each school has a unique approach, technique and philosophy, which it has passed down from generation to generation.

There are 6 major Ikebana schools which shall be considered individually in this section; these schools include:

1. Ikenobo School (Ikenobo-ryu)
2. Ohara School (Ohara-ryu)
3. Sogetsu School (Sogetsu-ryu)
4. Ichiyo School (Ichiyo-ryu)
5. Misho School (Misho-ryu)
6. Ryobi School (Ryobi-ryu)

Let us consider these 6 schools of Ikebana, one after the other.

1. IKENOBO SCHOOL

The Ikenobo school is one of Ikebana's oldest and most conventional schools. It was founded in the 15th century by a Buddhist priest, Senkei Ikenobo, at the Rokkakudo Temple in Kyoto, Japan. The Ikenobo school has played a major role in shaping Ikebana's techniques, principles, and aesthetics.

Some of the key features of the Ikenobo school include:

a. **Historical significance:** The Ikenobo school was founded in the Muromachi period and is one of the oldest schools of Ikebana. Senkei Ikenobo is notable for developing the art of Ikebana and formalizing its principles.

b. **Emphasis on line and structure:** The Ikenobo style strongly emphasizes creating elegant lines and structured arrangements. The arrangements under the Ikenobo school typically have a central vertical line (shin), a secondary line (soe), which slants diagonally, and a supporting line (hike) which forms a horizontal base.

c. **Harmony with nature:** The philosophy of the Ikebono school strongly emphasizes the harmony between nature and humans. Arrangements under this school aim usually communicate the natural beauty of plant materials and their surroundings.

d. **Use of seasonal materials:** Seasonality is vital in the Ikenobo school. Seasonal flowers, branches and foliage are usually meticulously chosen to mirror the time of the year. This practice finds its place in Japanese traditional values and aesthetics.

e. **The incorporation of Buddhism:** Senkei had a Buddhist background, which certainly influenced the Ikenobo school's approach to Ikebana. The practice of Ikebana was seen as a more spiritual activity than any other activity; it was seen as a form of meditation and a way to interact with the spiritual realm.

f. **Traditional forms and styles:** The Ikenobo school has preserved many traditional forms and styles of Ikebana that have been passed down from generation to generation. These forms and styles are usually symbolic and mirror cultural and historical contexts.

g. **Global impact:** The Ikenobo school has enjoyed an international spread with various branches and practitioners worldwide. This contributes to Ikebana's global recognition and appreciation as a distinct art form.

h. **Contemporary adaptations:** Although strongly rooted in tradition, the Ikenobo has adapted to modern insight and integrates contemporary elements into its arrangements.

Philosophy of the Ikenobo School

The Ikenobo school finds its roots in the philosophy that mirrors a profound appreciation of nature, harmony between man and the natural world, and a sense of spiritual connection. The historical context of the school, Buddhist influence and the cultural values of Japan all play a major role in its philosophy.

The following are integral aspects of the philosophy of the Ikenobo school:

a. **Respect for materials:** Reverence for each plant material used is a major aspect of the Ikenobo School of Ikebana philosophy. The school lays a lot of emphasis on the respect, appreciation and understanding of plant materials. It champions the understanding of the characteristics and symbolisms attached to plant material.

    b. **Reflection of the divine:** Another core aspect of the philosophy of the Ikenobo school is a connection with the divine. The act of flower arrangement is perceived as a means of connecting with the spiritual realm and expressing gratitude for the beauty of nature. Ikenobo practitioners typically approach Ikebana with a sense of reverence and spirituality.

    c. **Spiritual enrichment:** Flowing from the previous point is the aspect of spiritual enrichment that communicates the sense that Ikebana is an artistic endeavour and a route to personal and spiritual enrichment. The practice also encourages practitioners to develop an awareness of beauty, balance and harmony. The head of the Ikenobo school in the mid-16th century perfectly captured this aspect of the philosophy in the following words; "Not only beautiful flowers but also buds and withered flowers have life, and each has its beauty. By arranging flowers with reverence, one refines oneself."

    d. **Seasonality and temporariness:** The Ikenobo school also communicates the significance of using seasonal materials in the arrangement of flowers. This practice mirrors the Japanese cultural value of appreciating seasonal changes and being aware of the ephemeral nature of everything.

e. **Preservation of tradition:** Although the Ikenobo school is open to innovation and creative interpretation, it emphasizes preserving traditional Ikebana forms and styles. The rationale is that these forms and styles carry strong cultural and historical essence, passed down from generation to generation.

f. **Balance and unity:** Another important aspect of the Ikenobo philosophy is the search for a sense of balance, both spiritually and visually. The harmony in the arrangement of different plant materials and various lines and forms adds to a unified and balanced composition.

g. **Meditation and mindfulness:** Creating an Ikebana arrangement is usually perceived as a form of meditation and mindfulness. Practitioners of Ikebana develop a focused and present state of mind which allows them to connect with the creative process and the natural world.

2. OHARA SCHOOL

The Ohara School of Ikebana was founded in the early 20th century by Unshin Ohara as a response to Japan's evolving cultural and aesthetic sphere. The school is known for its unique approach to Ikebana, emphasizing space, naturalism and creative freedom.

The key aspects of the Ohara School of Ikebana are as follows:

a. **Naturalistic style:** The Ohara school is known for

its naturalistic and free-spirited style of Ikebana. Typically, arrangements under the Ohara school mimic the natural growth process of plants and capture their grace and elegance.

b. **Creative expression:** The Ohara School of Ikebana allows practitioners to combine creative juices and experiment with unorthodox materials. This approach to creativity deviates from the conventional schools that stick to more established principles.

c. **Moribana arrangements:** The Ohara school is known for popularizing the Moribana style, where arrangements are created in shallow containers using kenzan. The Moribana style gives room for more versatility in arranging and emphasizes depth and space.

d. **Use of space and emptiness:** The Ohara school also embraces the Ikebana concept of emptiness and typically integrates open space into its arrangements. The use of space communicates a sense of movement and calmness within the arrangement.

e. **Emphasis on learning:** The Ohara school places a premium on education and offers an organized curriculum for students to learn and master the different techniques of Ikebana.

f. **Seasons and natural elements:** Like other Ikebana schools, the Ohara school esteems the use of seasonal plant materials to emphasize seasonal changes and the beauty of nature.

g. **Contemporary adaptation:** Although it is constantly rooted in tradition, the Ohara school explores modern ideas and continues to evolve with them to create unique art forms.

h. **Global influence:** The innovative and adaptive style of the Ohara School of Ikebana has contributed to its popularity worldwide. It has caught the interest of various enthusiasts and practitioners around the world who value its contemporary approach.

Philosophy of the Ohara School

The Ohara School of Ikebana has a unique philosophy that esteems creativity, naturalism and deep interaction with the beauty and rhythms of the natural world. This philosophy has been key in shaping its distinct approach to Ikebana.

The following are key aspects of the philosophy of the Ohara school of Ikebana:

a.　**Embrace of natural beauty:** The Ohara school of Ikebana emphasizes reverence for the innate beauty of nature. Usually, arrangements under this school are created to capture the essence of natural forms and the organic growth process of plants.

b. **Three main principles:** The Ohara School of Ikebana is guided by three main principles; heaven, earth and man. Heaven represents the branches that reach upward; earth represents the horizontal elements; man represents the interaction between humans and nature.

c. **Connection to tea ceremony:** The Ohara school has a solid connection to the tea ceremony (chanoyu), where Ikebana arrangements add to the ambience and aesthetic experience.

d. **Spiritual sensitivity:** The philosophy of the Ohara school encourages practitioners to develop deep sensitivity to the natural world and to discover spiritual satisfaction through their arrangements.

e. **Evolution and innovation:** The philosophy of the Ohara school of Ikebana embraces change and evolution. This allows it to adapt to modern ideas while maintaining its core values and principles. It encourages Ikebana artists to explore modern ideas and techniques.

3. SOGETSU SCHOOL

The Sogetsu School of Ikebana was founded in the 20th century by Sofu Teshigahara and has become a prominent and innovative school. The school is notable for its experimental and modern approach to Ikebana and its emphasis on self-expression and creative freedom. Sofu Teshigahara aimed to break free from conventional constraints and make Ikebana accessible to people from all spheres of life.

The following are important features of the school:

a. **Creative expression:** The school focuses on creativity and artistic liberty. Practitioners are licensed to explore unorthodox materials, creative techniques, and artistic styles.

b. **Adaptability and innovation:** The Sogetsu school accommodates change and adaptation, which has allowed it to evolve with contemporary ideas and aesthetics. The school encourages practitioners of Ikebana to incorporate various arrangements and spaces.

c. **Non-traditional materials:** The Sogetsu school is notable for its openness to using various materials beyond conventional plant materials. It uses materials like metal, wire, fabric and even non-natural items. This approach gives room for a broad spectrum of design possibilities.

d. **Self-expression and individuality:** The school encourages individuality and personality in artistic expression, unlike other schools which adhere to specific forms. Ikebana arrangements are perceived as mirrors and extensions of the practitioner's emotions, experiences and interpretations.

e. **Sogetsu Ikebana everywhere:** The Sogetsu Ikebana

school pushes the idea that Ikebana can be practiced anywhere and by anyone without restrictions. Ikebana arrangements can be created for both traditional and unconventional settings, such as events and public spaces.

f. **Teaching and curriculum:** The Sogetsu School of Ikebana has an organized curriculum that accommodates beginners to advanced practitioners. Students are usually guided through various levels of skill development and encouraged to explore their unique creative paths.

g. **International reach:** The Sogetsu school has a massive international presence, with various branches and practitioners all over the world. Its contemporary and adaptive approach to Ikebana has caught the eye of a global community of Ikebana lovers.

Philosophy of the Sogetsu School

The Sogetsu school of Ikebana has a uniquely innovative philosophy that sets it apart from the conventional Ikebana schools. It emphasizes creative freedom, self-expression and the idea that Ikebana can be practiced anywhere and by anyone in the world.

The following are key aspects of the Sogetsu school philosophy:

a. **Artistic freedom and self-expression:** The core tenet of the Sogetsu philosophy is the belief in artistic freedom. Practitioners are motivated to express their uniqueness in creating Ikebana arrangements. In the Sogetsu school of Ikebana, arrangements are seen as a form of personal artistic expression or an extension of the personality or emotions of the practitioner.

b. **Emphasis on simplicity and minimalism:** While the

Sogetsu school embraces creativity and innovation, it also esteems the simplicity and minimalism of Ikebana arrangements. Even when using unconventional materials, arrangements typically maintain simplicity and balance.

c. **Individual growth and development:** The practice of Ikebana within the Sogetsu school is perceived as a path to personal growth and development. Practitioners are spurred to constantly learn, adapt and evolve their skills and artistic ideas.

d. **No restrictions:** The Sogetsu school firmly believes that Ikebana can be practiced in various settings and environments without the conventional limitations of Ikebana spaces. Practitioners of Ikebana under this school are encouraged to create arrangements for public spaces, galleries, homes and many unconventional locations.

e. **Inclusivity and accessibility:** The Sogetsu philosophy strongly stands on the claim that Ikebana should be accessible to people of all ages, backgrounds and skill levels.

f. **Unconventional materials:** The Sogetsu school is known for its enthusiasm to integrate a wide range of materials not considered conventional to Ikebana - for instance, paper, wire, fabric, and more. This approach opens up a new path to creative possibilities.

g. **Embracing change and innovation:** The Sogetsu school embraces change and innovation, which allows Ikebana to evolve with modern artistic ideas. Practitioners of Ikebana under this school are free to experiment with non-traditional materials, non-natural elements and modern design concepts.

h. **Relevance in modern life:** The Sogetsu philosophy

strongly advocates for the inclusion of Ikebana in modern life and settings. The school perceives Ikebana as a way to magnify the beauty of various places and moments.

4. ICHIYO SCHOOL

Ihei Ito founded the Ichiyo School of Ikebana in the 19th century, and has grown to be a unique and respected school of Ikebana. It is known for its graceful and minimalistic style that emphasizes the beauty of individual flowers and branches.

The following are key aspects of the Ichiyo school:

a. **Simplicity and minimalism:** The hallmark of the Ichiyo school is its emphasis on minimalism. Arrangements under this school are purposely kept simple, typically featuring just one of a few key elements.

    b. **Linear arrangements:** Arrangements under the Ichiyo school usually showcase linear and upright compositions. The school's emphasis on simplicity and elegance is mirrored in the clean lines and tidy designs.

    c. **Appreciation for imperfection:** The Ichiyo school of Ikebana aligns with the wasabi-sabi aesthetic in its appreciation of the beauty of imperfection, transience, and the natural cycle of life.

    d. **Focus on individual flowers and branches:** Unlike other schools that create extravagant compositions, the Ichiyo school emphasizes the intrinsic beauty of individual flowers and branches.

    e. **Seasonal sensitivity:** While simplicity is fundamental to this school of Ikebana, it still esteems the use of seasonal plant materials. Practitioners intentionally select materials that mirror the current season and the significance of nature.

f. **Preservation of traditional forms:** The Ichiyo school preserves traditional forms and techniques as it embraces minimalism and simplicity.

g. **Spiritual connection:** Ikebana under the Ichiyo school is usually perceived as a form of meditation and a way to connect with the deeper spiritual spheres of nature.

h. **Graceful and refined aesthetics:** The arrangements created under the Ichiyo school typically communicate refinement and elegance, accentuating the understated beauty of each element.

i. **Influence on modern Ikebana:** The Ichiyo school has had an unending impact on the development of Ikebana, spreading its influence to other schools and contemporary perspectives.

Philosophy of the Ichiyo School

The philosophy of the Ichiyo school centers on elegance, simplicity and the art of capturing the essence of nature. This philosophy is firmly rooted in Japanese aesthetics and cultural values.

Some of the core aspects of the Ichiyo philosophy include:

a. **The beauty of singular elements:** At the core of the Ichiyo philosophy is the belief that the innate beauty of a single flower or branch can have a powerful artistic voice. Practitioners endeavour to showcase the distinct qualities and characteristics of each element they work with.

b. **Linear and upright arrangements:** The Ichiyo school usually employs the use of linear and upright positions that communicate order and simplicity. These arrangements establish a sense of harmony and balance, mirroring the school's aesthetic principles.

c. Simplicity and minimalism: The Ichiyo school emphasizes showcasing the inherent beauty of individual flowers without excessive adornment. It focuses strongly on simplicity and minimalism in Ikebana arrangements.

d. **Natural refinement:** Ikebana within the Ichiyo school is notable for communicating elegance and grace. Arrangements are usually put together to communicate a feeling of subtle beauty that resonates with the viewer.

e. **Connection to nature:** The Ichiyo philosophy strongly emphasizes the connection between humans and the natural world. Ikebana is viewed as a way to appreciate and showcase the beauty of nature through artistic designs.

f. **Seasonal changes:** Practitioners of Ikebana under this school are sensitive to seasonal changes and incorporate the idea into their arrangements. They meticulously select flowers and branches that are appropriate for the current season.

g. **Protection of tradition:** the philosophy of the Ichiyo school encapsulates a profound respect for traditional forms and techniques of Ikebana.

h. **Reflection and contemplation:** Ikebana within the Ichiyo school is typically regarded as a reflective practice. Arranging flowers spurs practitioners to ponder on the fickleness of beauty and life.

5. MISHO SCHOOL

The Misho school was founded by Misho Myoo, a Buddhist Monk who desired to express the teachings of Zen Buddhism through the art of Ikebana. He integrated the Zen principles of simplicity and mindfulness into the art of flower arrangement. The Misho school is notable and influential for its emphasis on asymmetry, balance and the natural form of plant materials.

The following are integral to the Misho school of Ikebana:

a. **Naturalistic approach:** The Misho school appreciates the natural form of plant materials and captures their innate beauty without extreme manipulation. The arrangements under the Misho school usually emphasize the growth process and characteristics of flowers and branches.

  b. **Symbolism and harmony:** Ikebana within the Misho school typically communicates symbolic meanings that reflect Buddhist principles and Zen aesthetics. Arrangements are designed to evoke calmness, harmony and spiritual reflection.

  c. **Emphasis on asymmetry:** One of the integral characteristics of the Misho school is its emphasis on asymmetrical arrangements. Asymmetry is notable for reflecting the natural and spontaneous beauty found in nature.

  d. **Suiban arrangements:** Suiban refers to shallow containers filled with water and used for arranging flowers. The Misho school is known for using these containers to arrange flowers; arranging flowers in these filled containers creates the illusion of floating flowers.

e. **Reflection of imperfection:** Like the other schools inspired by Zen, the Misho school embraces the concept of wabi-sabi, finding beauty in imperfection, impermanence and the passage of time.

f. **Balance and movement:** While integrating asymmetry into its arrangements, the Misho school of Ikebana also embraces balance and progression. The use of space and negative space adds to a sense of unique balance.

g. **Connection to Zen Buddhism:** The philosophy of the Misho school of Ikebana is deeply rooted in Zen Buddhism, as it emphasizes impermanence, mindfulness and the beauty of simplicity.

h. **Contemporary adaptation:** While rooted in tradition, the Misho school has evolved with modern ideas, focusing on naturalistic beauty while embracing contemporary influences.

Philosophy of the Misho School

The Misho school has a profound philosophy that mirrors its connection to Zen Buddhism, its focus on asymmetry and its celebration of the natural beauty of plant materials. The philosophy is deeply rooted in simplicity, mindfulness and understanding the temporariness of things.

The following are core aspects of the philosophy of the Misho School:

a. **Zen aesthetics and mindfulness:** The Misho school draws a lot of inspiration from the principles of Zen Buddhism, emphasizing presence, mindfulness and a deep awareness of the present moment. Ikebana arrangements under this school are designed as a meditative practice which promotes inner peace and contemplation.

b. **Naturalistic harmony:** Ikebana under the Misho school aims to create harmony with the natural growth process of plant materials. Arrangements typically communicate the organic elegance and simplicity of plant materials.

c. **Wabi-sabi and impermanence:** The Misho philosophy syncs with the wabi-sabi aesthetic, which places great value on imperfection, temporariness and the beauty of the transient and humble. Furthermore, these Ikebana arrangements mirror the cycles of life.

d. **The essence of nature:** The school's philosophy captures nature's essence and spirit, going beyond mere presentation to trigger a deep sense of connection.

e. **Zen mind-heart unity:** The art of Ikebana is perceived as a way to create harmony between the mind and the heart, encouraging a deep sense of inner tranquility and clarity.

f. **Symbolism and contemplation:** The Misho school of Ikebana typically communicates symbolic interpretations that foster introspection and spiritual reelection. Ikebana is viewed as a way to express deep truths by arranging plant elements.

g. **Asymmetry:** Asymmetry forms a solid aspect of the philosophy of the Misho school. The philosophy revolves around the beauty of asymmetry and the elegant tension it births in arrangements. Asymmetry causes a sense of movement, energy and natural enthusiasm.

6. RYOBI SCHOOL

The Ryobi School of Ikebana is a unique and historically

significant school that has contributed to the evolution of Ikebana in Japan. It was founded by Sen'ei Ikenobo in the 17th century and is known for its distinct blend of traditional Ikebana principles and Chinese art and culture. Sen'ei Ikenobo was the 11th-generation headmaster of the Ikenobo school of Ikebana and desired to expand and diversify the artistic influences within Ikebana. Hence, the Ryobi school.

The following are key aspects of the Ryobi School of Ikebana:

a. **Chinese influence:** The Ryobi school draws some inspiration from the Chinese, incorporating elements of their painting, calligraphy and philosophy into Ikebana. This influence reflects in the school's arrangements which often include bold lines, elegant forms and a sense of movement.

> b. **Expressive use of space.** The school emphasizes the use of space within the arrangement. This is done by creating balance and harmony through the arrangement of plant materials and negative space.
>
> c. **Philosophical and aesthetic depth:** The philosophy of the Ryobi school is largely influenced by both Chinese and Japanese cultural and philosophical concepts. This adds a lot of depth and meaning to the arrangements in this school.
>
> d. **Preservation of tradition:** While integrating the Chinese elements, the Ryobi school also preserves a connection to traditional forms and flower arrangement techniques.
>
> e. **Bold and dynamic arrangements:** Ryobi arrangements are characterized by the dynamism communicated by their lines. These arrangements evoke a sense of vigor and vitality. Furthermore, they communicate some form of energy and progression, capturing the significance of nature's dynamism.
>
> f. **Seasonal sensitivity:** Like other Ikebana schools, the

Ryobi school is aware of seasonal changes and uses seasonal materials to reflect this.

g. **Historical and cultural context:** The Ryobi school came on board during the era of cultural exchange between the Japanese and Chinese. This has contributed largely to its distinct blend of influences.

h. **Influence on the Ikebana revolution:** Ryobi school's innovative perspective on Ikebana has contributed to the diversity and evolution of the art form.

Philosophy of the Ryobi School of Ikebana

As you would expect, the philosophy of the Ryobi school of Ikebana encapsulates a unique fusion of Japanese and Chinese influences. It combines traditional Ikebana principles with Chinese art, calligraphy and philosophical elements.

The following are core aspects of the philosophy of the Ryobi school of Ikebana:

a. **Fusion of cultures:** This is one of the most significant aspects of the school's philosophy. It is grounded in the blend of Japanese and Chinese cultures. The school draws inspiration from Chinese art forms and incorporates them into Ikebana.

b. **Symbolism and meaning:** under the Ryobi school, Ikebana typically communicates meanings and symbols relevant to Chinese and Japanese cultures and philosophies. Arrangements may communicate themes of spirituality, nature and the intersection between humans and the natural world.

c. **Dynamic expression:** One of the central principles of Ryobi philosophy is the expression of dynamic progression and energy in Ikebana arrangements. The arrangements are designed to communicate the energy and rhythm of nature, mirroring the influence of Chinese aesthetics.

d. **Harmony and balance:** The school lays a lot of emphasis on achieving balance and harmony within arrangements. Adopting bold lines and forms is meticulously balanced to create a sense of balance and beauty.

e. **Connection to nature and spirituality:** The practice of Ikebana within the Ryobi school is perceived as a way to interact with nature and develop a sense of spirituality. Arrangements are meant to evoke reflection and a deeper understanding of the natural world.

f. **Embracing change and evolution:** The Ryobi philosophy welcomes change and innovation while respecting the fundamental principles of Ikebana. It presents Ikebana as an art form which can integrate various influences.

g. **Cultural exchange and interaction:** This philosophy mirrors the historical context of cultural exchange and interaction between Japan and China.

The schools of Ikebana represent a wide range of Ikebana styles and approaches, each contributing uniquely to the art form's development. While each school has unique characteristics, they all share a unified foundation in Ikebana's fundamental principles – balance, harmony and a deep connection to nature.

CHAPTER TWO

MATERIALS AND TOOLS

"Ikebana is meant to mimic life in the way it develops; it shouldn't look like it's under the control of man."

-Camille Henrot

A lot has been discussed about Ikebana in the previous chapter, and I am pretty sure you gained a lot of things about Ikebana. It is time to build upon that foundation and talk about the materials and tools you need to be a practitioner of Ikebana.

A farmer never goes to the farm without his hoe, and a hunter never goes hunting for meat without his gun. Similarly, there are materials and tools a practitioner of Ikebana must have, without which they cannot practice the traditional Japanese art of flower arrangement. There are necessary tools which every practitioner or potential practitioner of Ikebana must possess to be successful in the craft.

Furthermore, it is important to note that the choice of materials and tools depends on the specific style and philosophy of Ikebana adopted.

This chapter focuses on these materials and divides them into 4 categories, namely:

      a.   Flowers and Plants

      b.   Vases and Containers

    c.   Scissors and Knives

    d.   Accessories

Each category will be delved into with adequate examples given. So, are you ready to take up your Ikebana tools to practice?

FLOWERS AND PLANTS

In Ikebana, the choice of flowers and plant materials play a vital role in birthing harmonious and aesthetically pleasing designs. Different schools and styles of Ikebana may go for different flowers and plants based on their seasonal availability.

The following are popularly used flowers and plant materials for Ikebana:

    a.   Pine branches (Matsu): In Ikebana, pine symbolizes longevity and resilience and is typically used as a central element within arrangements.

    b.   Cherry blossoms (Sakura): Sakura symbolizes the temporary beauty of life and is an important addition to Ikebana arrangements. It is typically used in spring.

    c.   Bamboo (Take): Bamboo represents strength and flexibility and is used for its elegant and vertical lines.

    d.   Chrysanthemums (Kiku): Kiku is also a common addition to Ikebana arrangements and represents longevity and autumn.

    e.   Peonies (Botan): Peonies are large lush flowers appreciated for their beauty and are commonly featured in spring and early summer Ikebana arrangements.

    f.   Plum Blossoms (Ume): Plum blossoms are appreciated for their early bloom in the latter part of winter. They represent endurance and hope.

    g.   Narcissus (Suisen): Narcissus flowers symbolize

renewal and the emergence of spring and are popular in arrangements created at the beginning of the year.

h. Iris (Ayame): Ayame is used for its vibrant color and distinct shape. The flower brings a touch of grace to Ikebana arrangements.

i. Orchids (Ran): Orchids are esteemed for their elegant appearance and are usually incorporated into modern and minimalist Ikebana styles.

j. Bamboo Grass (Sasa): The long slender leaves of Sasa are typically utilized to create movement and add dynamism to arrangements.

k. Japanese Maples (Momiji): Momiji has a distinctive shape and colorful foliage. It is a popular element for summer arrangements.

l. Camellias (Tsubaki): Camellias are popular in winter and early spring arrangements and are known for their simple and graceful petals.

m. Willow Branches (Yanagi): They are adored for their elegant and flowing appearance, often used to create cascading effects.

n. Tulips: Tulips come in a wide variety of colors and shapes and are very versatile, dynamic flowers.

o. Zinnias: Zinnias is a very vibrant flower and typically adds a pop of color and liveliness to Ikebana arrangements:

p. Rosehips: Rosehips add texture and attract interest to Ikebana arrangements.

The selection of flowers and plant materials should be largely based on seasonal availability, symbolism, and the unique mood or message of the arrangement. Undoubtedly, Ikebana fosters a celebration of nature's beauty and a harmonious fusion of various elements to create amazing art forms.

VASES AND CONTAINERS

Vases and containers play a very fundamental role in Ikebana as they serve as the foundation upon which Ikebana arrangements are created. They also add to the overall aesthetics of Ikebana arrangements.

Like the plant materials, the choice of vases and containers is greatly influenced by the style of Ikebana being practiced and the creative direction a practitioner wishes to take.

The following are vases and containers popularly used in Ikebana arrangements:

    a. Classic Ceramic Vases (Hanaire): Traditional ceramic vases are usually used in Ikebana to communicate a message of elegance and timeliness. These vases come in different shapes, sizes and glazes and can be used for traditional and modern Ikebana styles.

    b. Bamboo Baskets (Hanakago): Bamboo baskets are used to create arrangements to communicate a rustic and naturalistic vibe. They are typically used in the Ikebana style known as "Nageire."

    c. Shallow Dish (Suiban): Ther Suiban is a shallow, flat container used to hold water and is typically used for the Moribana style of Ikebana. It gives room for the creative use of space and creates an illusion of floating flowers.

    d. Glass containers: Clear glass containers introduce a modern and transparent arrangement base. This transparency allows the stems and water to become parts of the composition.

e. Hanging Vases (Kakehana): The hanging vases are usually suspended from above and are commonly used to display a single flower or branch. This creates a minimalist striking effect.

f. Metal vases: Metal vases like brass or copper can contribute to the sophistication and contemporary style of Ikebana arrangements.

g. Gourd vases: Vases created from dried gourds give a distinct and organic look that can add to the appeal of Ikebana arrangements.

h. Hanging Vessels (Tatebana): Hanging vessels are usually suspended vertically and are perfect for arrangements that emphasize vertical lines and movements.

i. Wooden Containers: Wooden containers give a warm and organic feel to arrangements. They are suitable for traditional and contemporary styles of Ikebana.

j. Ceramic Ikebana Pillars (Tawaraya): Tawaraya are cylindrical and are used to showcase individual flowers or branches with an emphasis on their verticality.

k. Stone or Ceramic Ikebana Plates: These plates are known to hold small individual arrangements or flower frogs and are often used to display multiple arrangements together.

l. Box Vases (Hakoire): These vases are used to create arrangements with an organized and geometric feel with a typical emphasis on clean lines and symmetry.

m. Ikebana Dishes (Kenzan-dai): Ikebana dishes are designed to contain kenzan (flower frogs) and offer a stable base for creating more vertically inclined arrangements.

n. Floating trays: These are designed to hold floating flower heads, petals or leaves, communicating a delicate and ethereal feeling.

In selecting a vase or container for Ikebana, it is important to consider the shape, size, colour and material in relation to the flowers and plants materials you plan to use. The interaction between the container and the arrangement is a significant factor in the practice of Ikebana, as it contributes to the beauty and balance of the composition.

SCISSORS AND KNIVES

Scissors and knives are vital tools for the practitioners of Ikebana as they use them to cut and shape plant materials with accuracy and care. Your choice of scissors and knives goes a long way in determining the quality of your arrangement.

The following are the types of scissors and knives commonly used in Ikebana:

Scissors

a. Hasami: These scissors are the most commonly used in Ikebana. They come with short, sturdy blades with a pointed tip; as a result, they are versatile for cutting different plant materials.

b. Bonsai shears: These shears have short, curved blades perfect for detail cutting and shaping branches and stems.

c. Usubasami: Usubasami scissors share some similarities with hanami scissors but have slightly longer and more slender blades. They are typically used for delicate cutting and shaping.

d. Bypass Pruners: These have two curved blades that bypass each other, making clean and accurate cuts. The bypass pruners are useful for cutting thicker branches.

Knives

a. Kanna (Ikebana Knife): The Kanna is a traditional Japanese knife with a thin, curved blade. It is used for trimming leaves and cutting stems at an angle.

b. Hassaku Knife: The Hassaku knife is a larger, curved knife used to cut thick stems and branches.

c. Ken (Bud Knife): This is a specialized knife used for accurately trimming leaves, buds and small stems.

d. Sekiha Knife: The Sekiha knife is versatile, with a sharp point and curved blade. Suitable for different cutting tasks.

In selecting scissors and cutting knives, it is important to carefully consider the type of plant materials you will use and the precision required for the Ikebana style you have chosen. Furthermore, ensure you keep your tool sharp and well-maintained to have clean cuts and reduce damage to plant materials.

The proper usage and care for your scissors and knives contribute to the artistry and craftsmanship of your Ikebana arrangements.

ACCESSORIES

Accessories in Ikebana are instrumental in adding uniqueness and enhancing the visual appeal of arrangements. Accessories can be incorporated depending on the Ikebana style adopted and one's degree of creative expression.

Below are common accessories used in Ikebana:

a. Suiban Liner: A Cuban liner is a removable container that keeps the main container clean. It can also be easily cleaned and replaced.

b. Floral Wire: Floral wire shapes and supports plant materials, giving you the freedom to create dynamic and creative forms.

c. Stones and Pebbles: Small stones and pebbles can be placed in the container to provide support and visual interest.

d. Mizuhiki: This is a type of traditional cord that is made from twisted paper. It can tie and secure plant materials and add a decorative element to arrangements.

e. Sand or Gravel: Sand or gravel can be used as anchors to hold plant materials in place. They also give a naturalistic feel to arrangements.

f. Tea Leaves or Moss: Tea leaves or moss can be used to cover the base of the container or create a natural, earthly background for the arrangement.

g. Decorative Paper: Colored or patterned paper can add accents, wrap stems, and creative decorative instruments within the arrangement.

h. Water-Soluble Dyes: Dyes can be added to the water in the container to give the arrangement a distinct and vibrant colour palette.

i. Mirrors or Reflective Surfaces: Mirrors or other reflective surfaces can be placed under the container to create an illusion of depth and magnify the visual effect of the arrangement.

j. Miniature Figurines or Objects: Small figurines, miniatures or symbols can be meticulously incorporated into the arrangement to convey some thematic meaning.

k. Decorative Pins or Picks: These accessories can be inserted into the arrangement to add interest and colour.

l. Candles or Lanterns: For special occasions, candles or lanterns can be incorporated to provide an intimate touch to an Ikebana arrangement.

A balance between the plant materials and the additional elements is a very key factor in pulling off the addition of accessories to your arrangement. The accessories should complement and enhance your arrangement rather than overwhelm it. Trying out different accessories can help you birth a unique and memorable Ikebana composition that mirrors your creative uniqueness.

CHAPTER THREE

TECHNIQUES AND STYLES/ TYPES

"The beauty of flowers is forever captured in the way floral designers make them a part of our life's memories,"

-Idalina Bertone

It is no news that Ikebana encapsulates a variety of styles and approaches, each with its own distinct techniques, principles and aesthetics. The basic styles of Ikebana often serve as a fundamental framework that practitioners can build on and adopt in line with their creative vision.

The basic styles of Ikebana include:

    a. Shoka Style

    b. Heika Style

    c. Rikka Style

    d. Moribana Style

    e. Nageire Style

    f. Jiyuka Style

Others include:

    g. Zen'ei Style

    h. Nana-bana (Seven Flowers) Style

Each style will be considered with emphasis on its individual uniqueness and significance.

SHOKA STYLE (FORMAL LINEAR ARRANGEMENTS)

The Shoka style of Ikebana is a traditional and formal Ikebana that originated in Japan in the 18th century (the Late Edo period). After its emergence in the Edo period, this style evolved into its current form in the late 19th century (Meiji period). The Shoka style is known for its emphasis on line and balance and the use of minimal materials to create graceful compositions. The style mirrors the great influence of Zen Buddhism and Japanese aesthetics, encapsulating principles of asymmetry, simplicity, and the beauty of imperfection.

Key Elements of the Shoka Style of Ikebana

a. Shin, Soe and Tai: Shoka arrangements usually involve 3 major branches or stems known as 'shin,' 'soe,' and 'tai.' These elements symbolize heaven, human and earth elements, respectively. Shin is the primary stem, soe complements the stem, and tai adds depth and fullness.

> **b.** Formal Upright Lines: Shoka focuses on adopting formal and upright lines, often achieved by positioning the shin, soe and tai in a triangular arrangement. The main stem is typically positioned vertically.

> **c.** Asymmetry: Shoka arrangements are intentionally asymmetrical and reflect the natural and imperfect beauty of the world. This contrasts with the symmetrical arrangements seen in some other styles of Ikebana.

> **d.** Container and Display: Shoka arrangements are usually displayed in a tall, cylindrical vase called a "shoka

hanaire." The vase is typically proportional to the height of the arrangement and is often chosen as a complementary element to the overall design.

e. Minimal Materials: Shoka arrangements commonly use a limited number of materials, emphasizing the essential elements to communicate the intended message or theme.

f. Negative Space: Shoka esteems the concept of "ma," or negative space, which is a key element in Japanese aesthetics. The arrangement of materials and empty space is meticulously considered to achieve harmony and balance.

g. Seasonal expression: Shoka arrangements usually incorporate seasonal plant materials, mirroring the shifting rhythms of nature and appreciating the beauty of each season.

h. Evolving styles: The style of Shoka has undoubtedly evolved over time, and today there are two main styles: "Shin" and "Gyo." The Shin style communicates a more traditional and rigid triangular form, while the Gyo style gives room for more creative expression and variation.

Shoka ikebana is usually taught in ikebana schools and is used in formal settings, ceremonies, and exhibitions. Apart from being a form of artistic expression, it is also a reflective practice that encourages practitioners to interact with nature and develop mindfulness. Shoka focuses on simplicity and balance, which makes it a timeless and meaningful style of Ikebana.

The core of the Shoka Style of Ikebana

At the core of the Shoka style of Ikebana is a set of principles and philosophies that guide the arrangement process and give the style its distinct character. These principles encapsulate the essence of Shoka ikebana and mirror its cultural, historical and aesthetic origins.

The following are some key aspects that constitute the core of the Shoka style:

    a.   Simplicity and Minimalism: Shoka esteems the beauty of simplicity by adopting a restricted number of plant materials. This approach shows the Japanese aesthetic of "less is more," giving each element the platform to be appreciated fully.

    b.   Triangular Composition: Shoka arrangements commonly align with a triangular composition, with the three main stems (shin, soe, and tai) creating the triangle's vertices. This structure births a sense of balance and stability.

    c.   Asymmetry and Imperfection: The Shoka style celebrates the concept of "wabi-sabi," which finds beauty in imperfection and asymmetry. Arrangements are purposely made to switch from strict symmetry to accepting the innate irregularities of nature.

    d.   Mindfulness and Reflectiveness: Creating a Shoka arrangement requires delicate observation, patience, and mindfulness. Practitioners of the Shoka style of Ikebana engage in a meditative process that connects them with the present and the beauty of the materials.

    e.   Harmony with nature: The Shoka style of Ikebana emphasizes a solid interaction and harmonious relationship with the natural world. Practitioners of this style seek to portray plant materials' intrinsic beauty and significance while revering their natural forms.

    f.   Cultural Heritage: The Shoka style of arrangement of flowers is deeply rooted in Japanese culture and traditions. Its principles and aesthetics mirror centuries of artistic and philosophical influences.

g. Adaptation: Undoubtedly, the Shoka style of Ikebana is deeply rooted in tradition; however, it has evolved over time to accommodate changing artistic ideas. Contemporary interpretations of Shoka preserve its core principles while allowing for creative freedom.

The core of Shoka ikebana spurs practitioners to explore the intersection between form, space, and materials while encouraging a sense of respect for nature and the temporariness of beauty it offers. Through the Shoka style, practitioners of Ikebana engage in a reflective and artistic journey that connects them with the significance of life and the world around them.

HEIKA STYLE (STEM-ARRANGED)

The Heika style of Ikebana is also known as the "Stem-Arranged" style. It is a contemporary and simplified approach to Ikebana that focuses on the beauty of individual plant materials and their natural forms. Heika is mostly considered a more relaxed and accessible style, which makes it a common choice for beginners and those seeking a minimalist aesthetic. The Heika style emerged in response to the complexity and formalism of traditional Ikebana styles.

Key Elements of The Heika Style of Ikebana

a. Simplicity and Gracefulness: Heika arrangements are characterized by their simplicity and grace. The use of minimal materials and trimmed design creates a sense of calmness and an understanding of beauty.

b. Choice of Containers: Containers used in Heika arrangements are usually simple and modest, which allows the focus to remain on the plant materials. Containers can be traditional or modern in design.

c. Creative Liberty: While Heika adheres to certain fundamental principles, it encourages creative freedom and experimentation. Practitioners can adapt the style to suit their unique artistic perspectives.

d. Balance and Proportion: Arrangements under the Heika style usually appear simple; however, they still align with principles of balance and proportion. The arrangements typically have a harmonious distribution of materials and a sense of balance.

e. Asymmetry and Naturalism: Heika adopts the concept of wabi-sabi, celebrating imperfection and embracing the natural irregularities of plant materials. Asymmetry is a common feature in Heika arrangements, giving them an organic and spontaneous vibe.

f. Seasonal Sensitivity: Like other Ikebana styles, Heika considers seasonal considerations. Practitioners usually choose plant materials that mirror the current season and improve the connection between the arrangement and nature.

g. Minimal Manipulation: Heika supports the minimal manipulation of stems and branches. Plant materials are arranged in such a way that their natural growth patterns and forms are preserved.

h. Negative Space: Just like in other Ikebana styles, Seika emphasizes using negative space to create a balanced and visually attractive composition.

i. Contemporary Adaptation: The Heika style has evolved over time and continues to be influenced by contemporary design aesthetics. Contemporary practitioners of Ikebana usually incorporate elements from other artistic disciplines, leading to diverse style presentations.

j. Focus on Individual Stems: Heika Ikebana emphasizes the distinct characteristics of each stem or branch used in the arrangement. The focus is on presenting the innate beauty of the plant materials themselves.

The Heika style of Ikebana presents a more accessible entry point into the world of Ikebana while still encapsulating the foundational principles of balance, harmony, and connection to nature. It's an ideal style for those who adore the beauty of simplicity and the meditative aspects of flower arranging.

The Core of The Heika Style of Ikebana

The core of the Heika style of Ikebana lies in its strong attention to simplicity, naturalism, and the intrinsic beauty of individual plant materials. This style aims to communicate the essence of nature and the distinctive character of each stem or branch while embracing the principles of balance and harmony.

The following are some key aspects that constitute the core of the Heika style of Ikebana

a. Celebration of Individuality: The Heika style esteems the distinct qualities of each stem or branch, allowing them to shine in their natural state. This approach sheds light on the inherent beauty of plant materials and celebrates their unique forms, colours, and textures.

b. Embrace of Imperfection: Heika style of Ikebana welcomes the Jaspanese aesthetic principle of wabi-sabi, finding beauty in imperfection and transience. Heika arrangements include elements that showcase the organic imperfection and asymmetry present in nature.

c. Asymmetry and Negative Space: Asymmetry is the trademark of the Heika style, contributing to a sense of dynamism and progression in the arrangement. Using negative (empty) space is important to create balance and visual agreement.

d.   Elegance: Heika arrangements are notable for their gracefulness and elegance, which creates an environment of simplicity and calmness around them. Using a balanced number of materials and tidy designs allows for reflection and an appreciation of each element.

e.   Creative Freedom: The Heika style of Ikebana embraces creative expression within the structures of its fundamental principles. Practitioners have the freedom to interpret the style in their own distinct way, resulting in various artistic expressions.

At its core, Heika ikebana encourages practitioners to connect with nature, develop mindfulness, and explore the beauty of simplicity. It offers a peaceful and reflective approach to flower arrangement, allowing beginners and experienced practitioners to engage meaningfully with the art form.

RIKKA STYLE (STANDING FLOWERS)

The Rikka style of Ikebana is notably one of the oldest and most traditional styles. It is known for its complexity, grandeur and symbolism. This style of Ikebana was developed in Japan during the old Muromachi period and encapsulated profound spiritual and philosophical meanings, as it equally represents the natural landscape. Rikka arrangements are known for their exquisite, multi-tiered structures and carefully arranged plant materials.

Key Elements of the Rikka Style of Ikebana:

a.   Symbolism and Harmony: Rikka arrangements are great symbols of the harmony that exists between man and nature. This reflects the Buddhist principle of interconnectedness. The Rikka arrangement style aims to recreate a natural landscape and integrate elements such as mountains, valleys and waterfalls.

b. Vertical and Horizontal Lines: Rikka places a lot of emphasis on vertical and horizontal lines to communicate height and balance. The main stems are arranged vertically, while the secondary stems are arranged horizontally to give the feel of a natural landscape.

c. Traditional Rules: Rikka follows a set of conventional rules that guide the arrangement's structure, proportions and symbolism. Practitioners of the Rikka style of Ikebana abide by these rules while giving room for creative expression.

d. Shin, Soe, and Tai: Like the Shoka style, Rikka uses three major elements; "shin" (truth), "soe" (supporting) and "tai" (mass). These elements are put together to form the structural foundation of the arrangement. They also represent the heavens, humanity and the earth, respectively.

e. Branch Manipulation: Under the Rikka style, plant materials and branches are meticulously manipulated and shaped to represent different features of landscapes. Techniques such as tate, also known as upright replacement, and kamae, also known as bending and arching, are used to achieve desired forms.

f. Seasonal Materials: Rikka arrangements integrate seasonal plant materials, mirroring the shifting beauty of nature throughout the year. Different flowers and branches are used to communicate the significance of each season.

g. Training and Mastery: Learning the Rikka style requires consistent training and mastery of specific techniques. Practitioners typically learn under experienced instructors to understand the complexities attached to balance, proportion, and symbolism.

h. Historical and Spiritual Significance: Rikka originally developed as an offering for religious ceremonies and rituals at Buddhist temples. It has a lot of historical and cultural significance as a form of artistic expression deeply rooted in Japanese spirituality.

i. Modern Adaptation: While Rikka remains attached to its traditional principles, contemporary practitioners have introduced variations and adaptations to the style. These adaptations reflect changing artistic ideas and give room for personal expression.

Rikka ikebana takes a special place in the history of Japanese floral art as it represents a deep connection between art, nature, and spirituality. The style's intricate designs, appreciation for nature, and symbolic meanings continue to inspire ikebana enthusiasts and showcase the depth of Japanese cultural heritage.

The core of The Rikka Style of Ikebana

The Rikka style of Ikebana is rooted in deep symbolism, spiritual significance, and meticulous craftsmanship. At its core, Rikka encapsulates principles that mirror a harmonious relationship between nature, humanity, and the divine. These principles influence the creation of elaborate and grand arrangements that symbolize the natural landscape in a stylized form.

The following constitute the core of the Rikka style:

a. Recreation of Nature: Rikka arrangements seek to recreate a stylized version of the natural landscape, typically depicting mountains, waterfalls, rivers, and valleys. The arrangement becomes a mini representation of the beauty and peace found in the natural world.

b. Balance and Proportion: Balance and proportion are

essential in achieving arrangements under the Rikka style of Ikebana. The arrangement is carefully organized, with each element contributing to the overall harmony. Practitioners follow specific rules and guidelines to distribute mass and form properly.

c. Seasonal Connection: Rikka arrangements integrate seasonal plant materials to communicate the essence of each season. This connection to the natural cycle emphasizes the arrangement's symbolism and relevance.

d. Spiritual Reflection: Designing a Rikka arrangement is a meditative process that encourages practitioners to ponder on the beauty of nature, the fickleness of life, and the interconnectedness of all things.

e. Master-Student Tradition: Learning the Rikka style of Ikebana usually entails a mentorship or apprenticeship under an experienced practitioner. The style's complexities and traditional rules are passed down through hands-on instruction.

The core of the Rikka style lies in its profound philosophical underpinnings, meticulous techniques, and the spiritual journey it offers practitioners. It embodies the essence of Japanese aesthetics, spirituality, and reverence for nature. All these make the Rikka style of Ikebana a captivating and culturally rich art form.

MORIBANA STYLE (PILED-UP FLOWERS)

The Moribana style of Ikebana is also known as the "Piled-Up Flowers" style and is a modern and versatile approach to floral arrangement that originated in Japan during the late 19th century. Unlike some of the more traditional and structured ikebana styles, Moribana gives an opportunity for greater freedom and creativity in arranging flowers and plant materials. This style is especially well-suited for showcasing a variety of materials and creating dynamic compositions.

Key Elements of The Moribana Style of Ikebana

a.   Naturalistic Perspective: Moribana embraces a more naturalistic presentation of plant materials, embracing their inherent shapes and forms. The focus is on capturing the beauty of flowers and branches as they would appear in their natural habits.

b.   Use of Different Heights: Moribana arrangements often integrate materials of different heights and a sense of depth and dimension. The layering of materials contributes to visual dynamism and lively composition.

c.   Piled-Up Composition: Moribana literally translates to "piled-up flowers," and the style emphasizes a natural, layered arrangement. Plant materials are arranged in layers, allowing them to intersect and overlap in an organic and visually captivating manner.

d.   Freedom of Expression: Moribana offers the arranger greater creative liberty than some other Ikebana styles. Practitioners can experiment with various angles, heights, and placements to achieve the desired aesthetic.

e.   Balance and Harmony: Although Moribana arrangements appear informal, they still abide by the principles of balance and harmony. The arrangement usually communicates a sense of equilibrium and visual appeal.

f.   Minimal Manipulation: Despite being a style that gives room for creative liberty, Moribana minimizes the manipulation of stems and branches. This is in contrast to more elaborate ikebana styles.

g.   Contrasting Textures and Colors: Moribana supports the use of different textures and colors to create contrast and visual appeal within the arrangement.

> h. Versatility: Another very interesting characteristic of the Moribana style is that it can be adapted to various settings and occasions, from casual and everyday displays to formal events and exhibitions.

The Moribana style of Ikebana allows practitioners to explore their artistic sensibilities as they work with plant materials' natural shapes and characteristics. It is a style that closes the gap between tradition and modernity, allowing for artistic expression and a deep connection to the beauty of nature.

The core of The Moribana Style of Ikebana

At the core of the Moribana style of Ikebana is a major emphasis on naturalism, artistic freedom and expression, and the dynamic intersection of plant materials within a shallow container. Moribana, meaning "piled-up flowers," offers a modern and versatile approach to floral arrangement that embraces the innate beauty of plants while allowing for artistic interpretation.

The following constitute the core of the Moribana style:

> a. Shallow Container (Suiban): The previous chapter has shed light on the concept of Suiban, so you are familiar with it. The use of a shallow container is a hallmark of Moribana. The Cuban allows for the layering and overlapping of plant materials and creates a sense of depth and complexity within the arrangement.

> b. Contrast and Balance: As it embraces creative freedom, Moribana follows the principles of balance and harmony. Contrasting textures, colors, and heights are meticulously considered to achieve a visually captivating and harmonious arrangement.

c. Interaction with Space: Moribana arrangements interact with the space around them, the container, and the surrounding environment. The arrangement's relationship with negative space is an important consideration at its inception.

d. Dynamic Layering: Moribana arrangements usually entail a layered and piled-up composition. There is usually an intersection between stems and branches, giving a visually appealing and three-dimensional effect.

e. Modern Interpretation: Moribana is a modern interpretation of the Japanese art of flower arrangement that embraces contemporary ideas as it maintains a connection to traditional principles of balance and aesthetics.

The core of the Moribana style spurs practitioners to appreciate the intrinsic beauty of plant materials, explore their artistic context and engage in a harmonious dialogue between nature, creativity, and space. It presents a distinct and lively approach to Ikebana that continues to evolve and captivate enthusiasts around the world.

NAGEIRE STYLE (THROWN-IN FLOWERS)

The Nageire style of Ikebana is also known as the "Thrown-In" style or "Tossing-In" style. It is an autonomous and expressive approach to flower arranging that originated in Japan. Unlike some of the more structured styles of Ikebana, Nageire gives room for a spontaneous and unrestrictive creative process. It involves placing plant materials in a vase or container in a natural, asymmetrical manner, often with a sense of progression and informality.

Let's consider some of the characteristics of the Nageire style of

Ikebana:

a. Spontaneity and Expressiveness: This is one of the most notable characteristics of this style, for obvious reasons. Who doesn't fancy some autonomy and spontaneity? Nageire presents a sense of spontaneity and freedom in arranging. Practitioners follow their guts and allow the materials to dictate the composition, resulting in unique and dynamic arrangements.

b. Minimal Manipulation: This style of Ikebana embraces a limitation in how plant materials are manipulated. Consequently, its manipulation of plant materials is minimal compared to other styles of Ikebana. The focus is on preserving the integrity of the stems and branches while allowing them to express their distinctive character.

c. Choice of Containers: It's no news that containers are foundational to any arrangement style; hence, they are integrated into this style. Containers used in Nageire arrangements vary widely, from conventional vessels to modern and unconventional options. Always remember that the choice of container can influence the arrangement's overall look and feel.

d. Creative Exploration: The Nageire style of Ikebana spurs practitioners to tap into their creative juices to bring out unique artistic forms. It supports exploring and experimenting with different combinations of plant materials, textures, and colors.

e. Negative Space: The Nageire style considers the use of negative space (empty space) as an integral element of the composition. There is no solid arrangement without employing the concept of negative space. The interplay between materials and empty space contributes to the arrangement's balance and aesthetics.

f. Informal Aesthetics: Even a non-human entity understands the need to go casual sometimes. Nageire arrangements have an informal and casual aesthetic. The goal is to evoke a sense of nature's spontaneity and how plant materials might naturally fall or intertwine.

g. Vertical placement: In the Nageire style, stems are placed vertically in a vase or container, often allowing them to lean or angle outward. This creates a sense of progression and adds to the arrangement's captivating quality.

h. Asymmetry and Naturalism: Nageire arrangements are purposely asymmetrical as they capture the organic and imperfect beauty of nature. The positioning of stems and branches reflects their natural growth patterns.

The Nageire style of Ikebana presents a refreshing shift from traditional rules and conventions, allowing practitioners to engage in more spontaneous and personal interaction with plant materials. It communicates the significance of nature's beauty and artistic enthusiasm, appealing to those who value creativity, individuality, and a sense of natural movement in their floral arrangements.

The Core of The Nageire Style of Ikebana

The core of the Nageire style of Ikebana is its emphasis on spontaneity, asymmetry, and the unrestrictive arrangement of plant materials. Nageire, meaning "Thrown-In" or "Tossing-In," encourages a free and intuitive approach to floral design. This style celebrates the beauty of nature in its organic forms and gives a platform for personal innovation and expression.

The following constitute the core of the Nageire style of Ikebana:

a. Spontaneous Creativity: The Nageire style of Ikebana esteems the spontaneous and intuitive creative process.

Practitioners are encouraged to let go of rigid rules and preconceived notions, allowing the arrangement to unfold naturally. Naturally, people can be more creative when not boxed into a corner and forced to abide by rigid rules. This style of Ikebana gives practitioners the freedom to spread their creative wings and "fly."

b. Seasonal Connection: Seasonal change is an integral aspect of the Ikebana art, as it communicates significance beyond the surface level. Despite its embrace of creativity, the Nageire style of Ikebana still incorporates seasonal plant materials. This practice adds depth and context to the arrangement, connecting it to the rhythms of nature.

c. Personal Expression: Nageire provides a platform for personal expression and individual creativity. Practitioners can experiment with different textures, colors, and forms to convey their artistic vision.

d. Contemporary Adaptation: The Nageire style of Ikebana has developed over time to accommodate contemporary ideas. Modern interpretations typically incorporate unconventional materials, design concepts, and innovative techniques, which has yet to take away the beauty of the Ikebana art form.

The central focus of the Nageire style is that it spurs practitioners to engage with nature's beauty in an unrestricted and authentic manner. It appreciates the intrinsic gracefulness of plant materials and introduces a direct, unmediated interaction with the natural world. Nageire Ikebana proves the power of spontaneity and the beauty that emerges when creativity is boxed into a singular direction.

JIYUKA STYLE (FREESTYLE)

Jiyuka is a term in Ikebana that refers to "freestyle" or "freestyle" arrangements. Unlike the traditional styles of Ikebana, which are guided by specific rules and principles, Jiyuka gives room for more creative expression and interpretation by the arranger. Jiyuka arrangements are not bound by strict guidelines, enabling practitioners to experiment with various materials, shapes, and design concepts.

The Jiyuka style is similar to the Nageire style as they are not bound by the strict guidelines that dictate the Ikebana art form.

Some main characteristics of the Jiyuka style of Ikebana include:

a. Creative Freedom: Creative freedom is the beauty that the Jiyuka style brings. Practitioners are given a free hand in expressing their artistic strengths and ideas. Jiyuka arrangements esteem creative freedom and individual expression. Practitioners are encouraged to follow their artistic instincts and create arrangements that resonate with their personal style.

    b. Non-traditional Materials: Many characteristics of the Jiyuka style of Ikebana send the message that it's probably a rebel style of Ikebana because it is not restricted like many other styles. However, that is the beauty of the style. Jiyūka allows for using unconventional or non-traditional materials in addition to flowers and branches. Practitioners can incorporate elements like fabric, paper, wire, and more.

    c. Form and Space: Jiyuka arrangements typically explore the interaction between form (the arrangement itself) and space (the empty areas around it). Negative space is used intentionally to improve the overall design.

    d. Inspiration from Nature: Although Jiyūka is freestyle, it still draws influence and inspiration from nature, seasons, or the surrounding environment. The natural beauty of plant materials is usually celebrated.

    e. Individual Style: Just like no two humans are the

same, the Jiyuka style presents various designs that are not the same. Each arrangement reflects the personality or orientation of the practitioner in charge of it. The Jiyuka style of Ikebana mirrors the arranger's style and preferences. Each arrangement is a unique artistic expression.

f. Minimal or Elaborate: The Jiyuka style presents a versatile approach to the arrangement of Ikebana. Arrangements can range from minimalist and simple designs to more elaborate and intricate compositions.

g. Open-mindedness: Apart from creative expression, another integral characteristic of the Jiyuka style is its openness to try many new things. It gives room for a lot of expression and experimentation. The style of Jiyuka encourages practitioners to explore new techniques, materials, and design concepts and supports innovation within the realm of Ikebana.

h. Contemporary Interpretation: Jiyūka embraces contemporary aesthetics and design concepts. It also integrates influences from various art forms and design disciplines.

i. Asymmetry and Balance: Although arrangements under the Jiyuka style of Ikebana do not abide by strict rules, they do not neglect principles of balance and asymmetry to create visually captivating compositions.

The Jiyūka style of Ikebana came on board due to evolving artistic orientations and the desire for greater artistic expression within the Ikebana tradition. It provides a platform for practitioners to break away from traditional constraints and explore the boundaries of their creativity, resulting in diverse, contemporary, and deeply personal arrangements.

The Core of The Jiyuka Style of Ikebana

The core of the Jiyuka style of Ikebana is plausible. If you have been following closely, you can predict this style's emphasis. The style emphasizes creative freedom, individual expression, and a break from traditional rules and restrictions. Jiyuka means "freestyle" or "free flowers;" it drives practitioners to break away from established norms and explore their unique artistic vision.

The following constitute the core of the Jiyuka style:

a. Innovation and Experimentation: Jiyūka encourages innovation and experimentation within the framework of Ikebana. Practitioners are free to explore new techniques, combinations, and concepts.

b. Individuality: The Jiyuka style champions wholeness, uniqueness and individuality. Each practitioner is able to bring their uniqueness to the table, which will reflect on the arrangements they design. Jiyūka arrangements are mirrors of the arranger's individuality and creative identity. Each arrangement becomes a unique representation of the practitioner's perspective.

c. Unrestricted expression: Jiyūka ikebana esteems untamed and unrestricted expression above all else. Practitioners are encouraged to follow their artistic instincts, allowing their personal vision and emotions to shape the arrangement.

d. Unorthodox materials: Jiyūka accommodates the use of unconventional materials beyond traditional flowers and branches. Practitioners can integrate many elements, such as non-botanical items, fabrics, metals, etc.

e. Modern aesthetics: The Jiyuka style of Ikebana embraces modern design ideas and gets inspiration from various artistic disciplines, including sculpture, architecture, and visual arts.

At the center of the Jiyūka style of Ikebana is its love

and celebration of the liberation of artistic expression within the context of Ikebana. It provides a solid foundation for practitioners to stand as they challenge conventions, push boundaries, and create arrangements that resonate deeply with their artistic sensibilities. Jiyūka Ikebana exemplifies the ever-shifting nature of artistic expression and reflects the diverse and contemporary interpretations of the Ikebana tradition.

The basic styles of Ikebana serve as platforms for the practitioners of Ikebana to explore and develop their skills. Each style offers its distinct artistic possibilities and cultural significance, allowing practitioners to express their creativity and engage with the aesthetics of Ikebana in diverse ways.

CHAPTER 4

ADVANCED TECHNIQUES IN IKEBANA

In the previous chapter, we explored the foundations of Ikebana, unveiling the secrets of its history, styles, and basic techniques. Now, in this chapter, we'll discuss the more advanced techniques. You can rest assured that you'll be greatly inspired as we journey through this road of endless possibilities, where emotions, colors, and shapes intertwine to create symphonies of beauty and meaning.

Each section in this chapter acts as a gateway to new dimensions of floral poetry. Get ready to unleash the full spectrum of your artistic prowess even as we travel together through the fusion of flowers and foliage, the creation of movement and balance, the vibrant use of color and shape, the harmonious incorporation of accessories, and the allure of seasonal Ikebana.

So, seize your heart's palette, pick up your virtuoso's baton, and let us journey together into the enchanting world of advanced techniques in Ikebana.

A. Combining Flowers and Foliage

First is the heartwarming embrace of combining flowers and foliage in the enchanting art of Ikebana. While flowers form the main component of Ikebana artistry, they are not the only elements that matter. By mastering how to combine flowers with foliage, you'll set your Ikebana arrangement in the highest of pedestals where floral artistry is concerned.

It's really so simple. But you have to bear the following points in mind before combining your flowers with foliage:

Embrace Diversity

Each flower and foliage is like a unique character in a grand theatrical performance. You must therefore embrace what makes them unique. For example, roses, proud and regal, can exude an air of elegance, but wildflowers, with their untamed spirit, have the capacity to add a touch of whimsy to your Ikebana.

One floral arrangement that has worked perfectly for me is the combination of red roses, daisies, and asters. How do you achieve a creative piece with these elements? Simply give your red rose the center stage it craves for and surround it with a wild profusion of daisies, asters, and baby's breath.

Both elements are known to communicate different emotions: Roses are a symbol of love and passion, while wildflowers are a symbol of carefree joy. Therefore, when you combine both together, you will create an arrangement that tells the story of love's blooming journey, where passion and freedom are evidently the order of the day.

Another combination you can try out is the merging of lilies with red anthuriums. Lilies give off vibes of serenity and represent purity and devotion. Anthuriums, on the other hand, exude passion and vitality. This arrangement becomes a narrative of balance, where the serenity of the lilies finds harmony with the fiery determination of the anthuriums, telling a tale of yin and yang in the art of floral expression.

Compose with Contrast

Contrast is the brush that paints emotion and intrigue in Ikebana. By bringing opposites together, you can achieve an orchestra of sensations and evoke a sensory symphony that stirs the soul.

For example, you can achieve an aesthetic Ikebana arrangement by marrying the tenderness of soft pink peonies with the strength of twisted branches. Peonies naturally embody grace and femininity, while twisted branches represent resilience and fortitude. This composition is a dance of contrasts—delicate blooms held aloft by rugged branches—an allegory of how strength and vulnerability intertwine in the human spirit.

Another floral-foliage combination that gels perfectly is an interswitch of rich, velvety hues of purple irises with the ethereal delicacy of baby's breath. There's one thing irises communicate to us with their beautiful appearance: wisdom and valor. Baby's breath, on the other hand, symbolizes innocence and purity because of how delicate they are. Can you guess what you get for combining both? You'll achieve a creation that could communicate a very inspiring message to the beholder:

"Even in life's darkest moments, there is a glimmer of hope and innocence,

creating a tapestry of emotions that moves the heart."

Weaving Foliage as a Tapestry

Foliage is the unsung hero of Ikebana! It brings out the very essence of your arrangement. Leaves have diverse shapes and hues that can serve as the foundation upon which your flowers take the grand stage.

You can play around this Ikebana masterpiece that showcases the vibrant crimson of geranium leaves, harmonizing with the velvety green of magnolia leaves. Many people see geranium leaves as a symbol of passion and intensity, while magnolia leaves could pose for strength and endurance. By bringing these two elements together, you'll create a masterpiece that communicates this motivational message to your viewers: *"Your human spirit is resilient. You can flourish even in challenging times!"*

Combining banana leaves with the feathery fronds of ferns also sounds like a bright idea. In this arrangement, your banana leaves will create a sense of grandeur and protection, while the fern fronds will evoke a feeling of airiness and movement. You can use this fusion of foliage to bring out the beauty of contrasts of: strength from the banana leaves and lightness from the fern fronds.

Unity in Diversity

The combination of flowers and foliage is like a symphony orchestra, and as the conductor of this floral symphony, you should strive for unity amidst the diversity. It is through unity that your arrangement can transcend the realm of a mere collection of blooms and foliage and transform into a harmonious tale that tugs at heartstrings.

To fully embrace diversity, you can try out this technique that melds the delicate purity of white calla lilies with the fiery energy of orange tulips. The calla lilies symbolize rebirth and purity, while the orange tulips represent passion and energy. In this arrangement, the unity lies in the shared purpose—the calla lilies embrace the tulips, mirroring how purity and passion harmonize, paving the way for a new beginning.

Examples of Flower and Foliage Combinations

You can try out these Ikebana arrangements on your own, and see how much magic lies within your reach.

Roses and Eucalyptus

- **Roses**: Symbolizing love and beauty, roses are available in various colors and represent a classic and timeless choice for Ikebana.

Having roses in this arrangement will make your Ikebana graceful.

- **Eucalyptus**: The aromatic and delicate foliage of eucalyptus complements roses beautifully. Considering the silvery-blue hues and refreshing scent of Eucalyptus will give your arrangement a sense of tranquility.

Irises and Sword Ferns

- **Irises**: Known for their elegant, sword-shaped leaves and striking blooms, irises symbolize faith, hope, and wisdom.

- **Sword Ferns**: With their tall, arching fronds, sword ferns add a sense of movement and grace to the composition.

Calla Lilies and Bear Grass

- **Calla Lilies**: Revered for their sleek, trumpet-shaped blooms and elegant lines, calla lilies represent purity and admiration.

- **Bear Grass**: The long, slender strands of bear grass add a sense of delicacy and lightness to the composition. Often used to create intricate looping and weaving effects, bear grass enhances the artistic flair of the arrangement.

Anemones and Olive Branches

- **Anemones**: Known for their velvety petals and bold, contrasting centers, anemones symbolize anticipation and protection. You can always count on anemones for a touch of drama and intrigue in your floral arrangements.

- **Olive Branches**: The silvery-green leaves of olive branches exude a sense of peace and abundance.

Sunflowers and Lemon Leaves

- **Sunflowers**: With their vibrant yellow petals and striking appearance, sunflowers convey a sense of happiness and joy. Because sunflowers are considerably large in size and bold in texture, they tend to stand out in this arrangement.

- **Lemon Leaves**: The glossy, bright green leaves of the lemon tree create a fresh and summery backdrop, enhancing the sunflowers' radiance and bringing a sense of zest to the composition.

Peonies and Ferns

- **Peonies**: Peonies speak of romance and abundance. Using them thoughtfully in any arrangement will give your Ikebana a more superior, lovey dovey look.
- **Ferns**: The delicate and feathery fronds of ferns add a touch of elegance and provide a soft, airy contrast to the lushness of peonies, contributing to the overall balance and harmony.

Tulips and Pussy Willow Branches

- **Tulips**: These graceful and vibrant flowers symbolize elegance and springtime. Tulips have slender stems and elegant blooms that can make the composition simple and more refined
- **Pussy Willow Branches**: The soft and fuzzy catkins of pussy willow branches create an intriguing contrast to the smooth petals of tulips. Unlike Tulips, pussy willow branches can invoke a playful and whimsical touch to this composition.

Lilies and Hosta Leaves

- **Lilies**: Known for their dramatic and exotic appearance, lilies exude a sense of sophistication and purity.
- **Hosta Leaves**: While lilies win the height game, hosta plants come bearing broad and striking leaves that offer a solid and structural foundation for this design. Hosta leaves have bold green hues that complement the graceful lilies perfectly and provide a sense of stability to the arrangement.

Orchids and Bamboo

- **Orchids**: Exotic and graceful, orchids symbolize beauty, luxury, and refinement.
- **Bamboo**: The tall and slender bamboo stems evoke the spirit of Japan and create a sense of harmony and simplicity. Bamboo stems have signatory vertical lines that are very visible, and can add a natural and calming effect to this composition.

Daisies and Dusty Miller

- **Daisies**: Representing innocence and simplicity, daisies are cheerful and versatile flowers that can be used to convey a relaxed and casual atmosphere in an arrangement.
- **Dusty Miller**: The silvery, fuzzy foliage of dusty miller brings a touch of elegance and vintage charm to the daisies.

Carnations and Aspidistra Leaves

- **Carnations**: Long-lasting and available in a wide range of colors, carnations are a budget-friendly choice that offers texture and variety to the arrangement.
- **Aspidistra Leaves**: With their broad, glossy leaves, aspidistra provides a bold backdrop for the delicate carnation blooms. Thanks to their deep rich color, this composition will be graced with depth and contrast.

Hydrangeas and Nandina Berries

- **Hydrangeas**: Symbolizing gratitude and heartfelt emotions, hydrangeas boast voluminous, globe-like blooms that add fullness and substance to an arrangement.
- **Nandina Berries**: The colorful and delicate berries of the nandina shrub add a touch of whimsy and autumnal charm to the hydrangeas, creating an interesting interplay of shapes and colors.

Chrysanthemums and Maple Leaves

- **Chrysanthemums**: Chrysanthemums symbolizes longevity and abundance and could make for striking focal points with their intricate petals.
- **Maple Leaves**: As a representation of autumn and change, maple leaves add a burst of vibrant colors to the arrangement. Maple leaves have a detailed and textured appearance that tends to bring a sense of mobility and liveliness to this composition.

B. Creating Movement and Balance

Now that you have mastered the art of combining flowers and foliage, we move further to another advanced Ikebana technique, where movement and balance take the grand stage in your design.

Embrace the Flow

Within the heart of every captivating Ikebana arrangement lies a sense of flow that guides the eye and soul alike. To understand how to embrace the flow in your design, you must understand the concept of *Ma*.

In Ikebana, the term *Ma* encapsulates the idea of negative space or the empty areas between flowers in an arrangement. Ikebana artists use *Ma* to achieve a delicate balance by leaving deliberate spaces in their arrangement.

You can practice how to incorporate the concept of *Ma* in your Ikebana design using slender reeds and delicate orchids thoughtfully. In this combination, the empty spaces between the two components will hold the essence of tranquility and anticipation. Each element will compliment the other perfectly.

Another creative idea could involve capturing the vibrant energy of a cascading waterfall. This can be achieved by letting long, flowing stems of irises and ferns spill over the container's edge and allowing the negative space to mirror the calm pool beneath the cascades. The movement in this arrangement captures the dynamic essence of nature's unstoppable force, evoking a sense of awe and admiration.

Find Equilibrium

The art of visual equilibrium lies at the core of every captivating Ikebana arrangement. Whether you choose a symmetrical, asymmetrical, or radial design, the key is to strike a perfect balance that soothes the eye and evokes a profound sense of peace. You must master the art of orchestrating the placement of your design elements to create a harmonious composition.

A classic example of equilibrium in Ikebana involves using a single lily at the center of an arrangement, flanked by an equal number of delicate chrysanthemums on each side. This harmonious arrangement evokes a sense of calm and order.

To understand this concept further, you can also take cues from this Ikebana design where a cluster of roses and wildflowers bursts forth on one side, while a lone branch with delicate leaves reaches towards the heavens on the other.

Capture Movement

Emotion in motion—weaving this enchanting essence into your Ikebana arrangement will elevate your design to aesthetic heights.
By mastering the art of capturing movement, viewers will be drawn towards being a part of your design. Each element within your arrangement will be allowed to tell a unique story of growth.

See the following inspirations:

- An Ikebana arrangement that embodies the essence of a whirling dervish, with twirling stems of calla lilies and heliconias creating a sense of spiraling motion. This creative piece will invite the most laid back viewer to see the genius you have created.

- A design that captures the delicate movement of a field of poppies gently swaying in the breeze. The slender poppy stems will come alive with each passing breath of air and evoke a sense of serenity and grace to your surrounding.

Harmonizing Colors and Textures

The concept of harmonizing colors and textures will make your painter's palette come alive in Ikebana. Simply put, you can use colors and textures to create captivating compositions by carefully choosing your bloom and foliage for its unique hue and tactile quality.

Be inspired by these arrangements:

- An Ikebana design that fuses the soft petals of pink peonies with the velvety leaves of lamb's ear and the smooth, glossy stems of magnolia. This harmonious blend of colors and textures results in a masterpiece that caresses both the eyes and the fingertips, like the delicate touch of a gentle breeze on a summer's day.
- An arrangement that marries the fiery red of maple leaves with the rough bark of birch branches. The contrasting colors and textures create a sense of harmony that celebrates the changing seasons, akin to the lyrical beauty of nature's transition.

Notable Arrangements that Create Movement and Balance

You can try out each of these combinations to achieve movement and balance in your design:

Roses and Baby's Breath

Baby's breath adds a delicate touch to the majestic roses, creating an ethereal and romantic ambiance. Be sure to position the roses and baby's breath in a way that complements each other, forming a balanced and graceful display.

Orchids and Snake Grass

The elegant orchids are perfectly complemented by the slender, sinuous snake grass. Allow the snake grass to gently intertwine with the orchids, creating a harmonious dance of forms and lines.

Lilies and Ruscus Leaves

Embrace the regal beauty of lilies by pairing them with the lush, glossy ruscus leaves. Place the lilies in between the ruscus leaves to create a serene and balanced environment that highlights their grandeur.

Sunflowers and Wheat Stalks
Combine the radiant sunflowers with the rustic charm of wheat stalks. Put them in such a way that showcases the sunflowers' cheerful faces while embracing the organic quality of the wheat stalks.

Carnations and Ivy Vines
Carnations exude their charm when accompanied by the elegant ivy vines. Allow the ivy vines to meander gracefully around the carnations, providing a sense of connection and unity.

Tulips and Bear Grass
Emphasize the elegance of tulips by pairing them with the slender, flexible bear grass. Allow the bear grass to weave gently between the tulips, creating a balanced and visually appealing composition.

Hydrangeas and Plum Blossoms
The lush hydrangeas find harmony with the delicate beauty of plum blossoms. Intertwine the plum blossoms amidst the hydrangeas to create a poetic and serene arrangement.

Chrysanthemums and Bamboo
The timeless allure of chrysanthemums can be combined with the sturdy elegance and traditional look of bamboo. Arrange the chrysanthemums alongside the bamboo, embodying a sense of strength and serenity.

Daisies and Goldenrod
Pair the cheerful daisies with the vibrant goldenrod for a lively and colorful display. Allow the goldenrod to accentuate the daisies, providing a burst of energy to the arrangement.

Irises and Fern Fronds
Embrace the allure of irises by complementing them with the delicate beauty of fern fronds. Allow the fern fronds to frame the irises gracefully, creating a composition that exudes serenity and charm.

Calla Lilies and Dracaena Leaves
Highlight the sophistication of calla lilies by pairing them with the

sleek dracaena leaves. Position the dracaena leaves to form an elegant backdrop for the calla lilies, fostering a sense of refinement.

Anemones and Seeded Eucalyptus
Create an enchanting atmosphere by combining the captivating anemones with the textured seeded eucalyptus. Allow the seeded eucalyptus to add a soft and romantic touch to the arrangement.

Peonies and Dusty Miller
The opulent peonies find harmony with the silvery foliage of dusty miller. Intersperse the dusty miller amidst the peonies, lending a touch of sophistication and timelessness.

Nigella (Love-in-a-Mist) and Willow Branches
Embrace the enchanting quality of nigella by pairing it with the graceful willow branches. Allow the willow branches to gently sway among the nigella, creating a dreamy and whimsical display.

Gerbera Daisies and Asparagus Fern
Celebrate the vibrant hues of gerbera daisies by pairing them with the feathery asparagus fern. Position the asparagus fern to provide a soft and lush backdrop for the gerbera daisies, creating a lively and cheerful arrangement.

Use these inspirations as a motivation to embrace the flow of your arrangement, find equilibrium, capture movement, and harmonize colors and textures because within these principles lies the very soul of Ikebana's allure.

C. Using Color and Shape

Color and shape are two of the strongest backbones of any Ikebana arrangement. No Ikebana design can pass the eye test if it doesn't have an excellent color and shape incorporation.

These two elements hold the key to how much viewers will appreciate your craft. An Ikebana design without a perfect blend of color and shape is like Thanos with an empty Infinity Gauntlet.

By understanding how to use color and shape in your Ikebana arrangements, you'll hold in your hands the very essence of an artistic experience that goes beyond the boundaries of the visual and reaches deep into the depths of the soul.

The Language of Color

Colors take on a life of their own in Ikebana, each one resembling the very notes that compose the enchanting melody of your arrangement. Each hue carries a unique resonance, eloquently speaking to the heart in a language that surpasses words. The warm reds ignite the flames of passion, the cool blues serenade the soul with tranquility, the sunny yellows radiate vivacity and joy, and the earthy browns resonate with a sense of grounded strength and stability.

To understand this concept perfectly, I want you to picture an Ikebana arrangement ablaze with fiery reds and oranges, symbolizing the intensity of a roaring fire on a cold winter's night. Or try to imagine a serene composition of cool blues and purples, a tranquil reflection of a moonlit lake in the stillness of the night. Now, envision a bouquet of sunny yellows, capturing the essence of a sun-kissed morning in a field of wildflowers. What's the common denominator in these arrangements? A thoughtful combination of colors and shape.

You too can joyously enchant your viewers by color in Ikebana.

Examples of Color and Shape Combinations

Be inspired by these color and shape combinations for your Ikebana arrangement

White Calla Lilies and Red Roses

The elegant, curving form of white calla lilies complements the lush, romantic shape of red roses, creating a visually striking contrast.

Purple Irises and Yellow Daffodils

The tall, sword-like shape of purple irises pairs beautifully with the trumpet-like form of yellow daffodils, resulting in an arrangement that exudes energy and elegance.

Orange Gerbera Daisies and Blue Delphiniums

The round, cheerful faces of orange gerbera daisies balance well with the tall, spiky appearance of blue delphiniums, adding dynamic visual interest.

Pink Peonies and Green Bells of Ireland

The luxurious, layered petals of pink peonies harmonize with the tall, columnar shape of green bells of Ireland, achieving a blend of softness and structure.

Yellow Sunflowers and Purple Statice

The vibrant, sun-like appearance of yellow sunflowers complements the clustered, cloud-like shape of purple statice, resulting in an arrangement that feels both bold and delicate.

Pink Ranunculus and White Queen Anne's Lace

The intricate layers of pink ranunculus blend elegantly with the delicate, lacy appearance of white Queen Anne's lace, achieving a romantic and ethereal feel.

Red Dahlias and Yellow Billy Balls

The bold, petal-filled structure of red dahlias contrasts with the cheerful, spherical form of yellow billy balls, creating an arrangement that's full of personality.

Lavender Hydrangeas and Green Viburnum The lush, rounded clusters of lavender hydrangeas pair charmingly with the globe-like clusters of green viburnum, offering a sense of abundance and symmetry.

Blue Hyacinths and White Freesias

The tall, fragrant spikes of blue hyacinths complement the delicate, funnel-shaped blooms of white freesias, resulting in an arrangement that's both visually appealing and aromatic.

Orange Marigolds and Purple Asters

The vibrant, multi-petaled appearance of orange marigolds finds a complementary partner in the star-like shape of purple asters, bringing an energetic and cheerful vibe to your arrangement.

The Art of Incorporating Accessories

Ikebana, a captivating art form that unites nature and human expression, has the capacity to stir the deepest emotions within us. As you stand before an arrangement, you're not just arranging flowers; you're weaving a symphony of feelings, memories, and aspirations into a living masterpiece. The addition of accessories takes this artistic experience to another realm, where the beauty of nature converges with the human touch.

Adornments

Accessories are the dazzling gems that add sparkle and charm to your arrangements. Like twinkling stars in a moonlit sky, these delightful additions elevate your floral poetry to celestial heights, where each element shines with its own brilliance.

In the pursuit of creating arrangements that captivate the heart and stir the soul, you must learn to embrace the joyful art of selecting accessories. Think of them as treasured companions, each with its own unique voice, adding depth and meaning to your floral masterpieces.

Searching for the best accessories is one captivating adventure that can be really rewarding. Just as a master chef seeks the finest ingredients to create a sumptuous feast, allow your creativity to roam freely as you peruse the vast palette of Ikebana accessories.

There are many accessories that can be incorporated into your designs, some of which can take your Ikebana to the next level. You will discover an array of ribbons, gemstones, and figurines that beckon your artistic touch. From the subtle elegance of a crystal bead garland to the whimsy of delicate figurines, each accessory carries its own charm, waiting to be woven into the fabric of your artistic vision.

In your search for adornments, ensure to let your imagination soar like a spirited butterfly, dancing from one captivating accessory to another. Experiment with the interplay of colors, textures, and shapes, like a painter mixing hues on a vibrant canvas. Allow your heart to be your guide, for within its depths lies the key to curating a symphony of accessories that resonates with the essence of your arrangement.

See yourself as the storyteller, and each accessory as a character in the tale of your Ikebana arrangement. From the delicacy of a single feather to the grandeur of a vintage pocket watch, the accessories you choose carry with them a rich symbolism that deepens the narrative of your creation.

Ikebana Accessories that Can Enhance Your Design

Vase

The journey begins with the selection of a vase—the vessel that will cradle your creation. This seemingly simple decision holds the power to evoke emotions and set the tone for your Ikebana design.

Ensure to consider size, shape, and aesthetics when considering your flower vase. It is very important you select a vase that perfectly complements your arrangement.

Whether you are aiming for traditional elegance or you want a more modern feel, there's a vase that fits your artistic expression. You can try out any of these options:

1. **Moribana Vase**:
    - Low and wide design.
    - Ideal for creating landscapes and shallow arrangements.
    - Allows for arranging flowers at different heights.

2. **Nageire Vase**:
    - Tall and upright shape.
    - Best suited for creating dynamic and graceful arrangements.
    - Emphasizes the natural flow of stems and branches.

3. **Shoka Vase**:
    - Triangular form with a narrow neck.
    - Perfect for traditional Shoka-style arrangements.
    - Helps achieve balanced compositions with emphasis on line and harmony.

4. **Suiban (Water Basin) Vase**:
    - Flat and shallow container.
    - Used for arrangements with water and floating elements.
    - Creates a serene and reflective atmosphere.

5. **Moribana Heika Vase**:
    - Combination of Moribana and Nageire styles.
    - Allows for a variety of arrangements by adjusting the vase's height and depth.
    - Provides flexibility in showcasing different floral elements.

6. **Rikka Vase**:
    - Elongated and slender design.
    - Specifically designed for the intricate Rikka style.
    - Accommodates the complex hierarchy of elements in Rikka arrangements.

7. **Jiyūka or Freestyle Vase**:
    - Unconventional shapes and designs.
    - Encourages creative expression and experimentation.
    - Perfect for contemporary interpretations of Ikebana.

8. **Hanaire Vase**:
    - General term for flower vases.
    - Available in various shapes, sizes, and materials.
    - Used for various Ikebana styles, depending on the arrangement's theme.

9. **Usubata Vase**:
   - Wide, shallow, and open vessel.
   - Often made of metal or ceramics.
   - Suitable for bold and impactful arrangements.

10. **Hanakago Vase**:
    - Woven basket-style vase.
    - Adds a rustic and traditional touch to Ikebana.
    - Perfect for informal and countryside-inspired arrangements.

11. **Nagaire Upright Vase**:
    - A variation of the Nageire style.
    - Characterized by a straighter and more upright design.
    - Supports tall and majestic arrangements.

12. **Moribana Nageire Vase**:
    - Combines elements of both Moribana and Nageire styles.
    - Allows for diverse arrangements that blend low and high elements.
    - Provides a unique and harmonious look.

13. **Rimpa-style Vase**:
    - Inspired by the Rimpa school of Japanese art.
    - Often features intricate designs and decorations.
    - Enhances the visual appeal of the Ikebana arrangement.

14. **Hanaikada Vase**:
    - Features a wavy or undulating rim.
    - Adds a sense of movement and liveliness to the arrangement.
    - Suitable for both traditional and modern Ikebana designs.

15. **Modern Minimalist Vase**:
    - Simple and sleek designs.
    - Emphasizes the beauty of individual floral elements.
    - Aligns well with contemporary and minimalist Ikebana styles.

16. **Tsuri-kake Hanging Vase**:
    - Suspended or hanging design.
    - Adds a dynamic and unconventional element to Ikebana.
    - Allows for arrangements that interact with the surrounding space.

Complementary Colors

Emotions are intricately tied to colors, and colored accessories offer a chance to amplify these emotions. Here are some complementary color examples that can amplify your Ikebana arrangement:

1. **Red and Green**
   - Classic complementary pair.
   - Creates a lively and eye-catching contrast.
   - Use various shades of red and green for depth and balance.

2. **Blue and Orange**
   - Bold and striking combination.
   - Adds a dynamic and energetic feel to the arrangement.
   - Experiment with different shades of blue and orange.

3. **Purple and Yellow**
   - Elegant and regal contrast.
   - Creates a harmonious yet attention-grabbing effect.
   - Choose rich purples and vibrant yellows for a captivating arrangement.

4. **Pink and Teal/Aqua**
   - Soft and serene combination.
   - Adds a touch of tranquility and modernity to the arrangement.
   - Play with pastel pinks and muted teal tones.

5. **Magenta and Lime Green**
   - Playful and vibrant contrast.
   - Creates a sense of whimsy and liveliness.
   - Opt for intense magenta and bright lime green for a cheerful arrangement.

6. **Crimson and Turquoise**
   - A unique and eye-catching pair.
   - Balances warmth and coolness for a visually engaging result.
   - Utilize deep crimson and turquoise for a dramatic effect.

7. **Burgundy and Chartreuse**
   - Rich and luxurious contrast.
   - Adds sophistication and opulence to the arrangement.
   - Experiment with deep burgundy hues and lively chartreuse shades.

8. **Lavender and Gold**
   - Delicate and refined combination.
   - Infuses a touch of elegance and glamor.
   - Choose soft lavender tones and shimmering gold accents.

Ribbons and Bows

Ribbons and bows have an innate ability to add a touch of grace and playfulness to your Ikebana creations. A simple silk ribbon tied around the neck of a vase can transform it into an exquisite masterpiece. Choose ribbons that match your arrangement's color palette or introduce a complementary hue to enhance the overall appeal.

Pendants or Charms

Incorporating pendants or charms into your Ikebana is like weaving a piece of your heart into every bloom. Attach a small pendant or charm to the vase or intertwine it with the flower stems. Choose symbols that hold personal significance—a locket with a picture, a miniature heart, or a meaningful trinket.

Decorative Stones

The addition of decorative stones or pebbles at the base of your Ikebana arrangement can ground it in a natural setting. Select stones that complement your arrangement's colors and textures.

You can incorporate any of these precious stones into your Ikebana:
1. **River Rocks**
    - Smooth and natural stones found in rivers and streams.
    - Come in various sizes and colors, including shades of gray, beige, and brown.
    - Offer a serene and organic look to your arrangement.

2. **Polished Pebbles**
    - Small, rounded stones that have been polished for a smooth surface.
    - Available in a wide range of colors, from neutrals to vibrant shades.
    - Add a touch of elegance and shine to your arrangement.

3. **Colored Glass Stones**
    - Translucent glass stones in assorted colors.
    - Reflect light and add a pop of color to your Ikebana.
    - Ideal for contemporary and creative arrangements.

4. **Black Basalt Stones**
    - Dark and angular stones that create a dramatic contrast.
    - Often used to evoke a sense of Zen and tranquility.
    - Suitable for minimalist and modern arrangements.

5. **Crystal Quartz**

- Clear or slightly tinted quartz crystals.
- Bring a touch of sparkle and mystique to your arrangement.
- Can add an ethereal quality to your Ikebana.

6. **Jade Stones**
   - Smooth, green stones that evoke a calming ambiance.
   - Work well in arrangements with natural or tranquil themes.
   - Symbolize good luck, protection, and harmony.

7. **Amethyst Geodes**
   - Semi-precious stones with vibrant purple hues.
   - Bring a sense of luxury and spirituality to the arrangement.
   - Create an eye-catching focal point.

8. **Slate Chips**
   - Flat, irregular pieces of slate in earthy tones.
   - Offer a rustic and natural appearance.
   - Suitable for arrangements with a countryside or outdoor vibe.

9. **Marble Chips**
   - Polished marble stones in various colors.
   - Convey a sense of refinement and elegance.
   - Ideal for arrangements with a classical or opulent theme.

10. **Ceramic or Porcelain Stones**
    - Man-made stones with intricate patterns and designs.
    - Add an artistic touch to your Ikebana arrangement.
    - Perfect for arrangements that celebrate craftsmanship.

11. **Hematite Stones**
    - Metallic gray-black stones with a reflective surface.
    - Add a touch of sophistication and depth to your arrangement.
    - Symbolize protection, grounding, and harmony.

12. **Lapis Lazuli Stones**
    - Deep blue stones with gold flecks.
    - Bring a sense of royalty, wisdom, and spirituality.
    - Add a regal touch to your Ikebana design.

13. **Agate Slices**
    - Thin, translucent slices of agate in various colors.
    - Create a mesmerizing effect with their natural patterns.
    - Can serve as elegant and unique bases for floral elements.

14. **Tiger's Eye Stones**
    - Brown-gold stones with a distinctive chatoyant effect.

- Evoke a sense of strength, confidence, and protection.
- Add a touch of warmth and energy to your arrangement.

15. **Coral Stones**
    - Naturally formed coral pieces in various sizes.
    - Bring a touch of the ocean and marine life to your arrangement.
    - Symbolize protection, healing, and vitality.

Dried Leaves or Twigs

Integrate dried leaves or twigs to celebrate the beauty of each season. Whether it's the rustling leaves of autumn or the delicate twigs of winter, these accessories bring the ever-changing natural world into your Ikebana. As you select leaves and twigs, consider their colors and shapes, letting them tell a story of time passing through the canvas of your arrangement.

Beads or Gems

Stringing beads or gems along the stems of your flowers creates a luxurious aura within your Ikebana. The play of light against these embellishments adds a glistening opulence, catching the viewer's eye and guiding their gaze through the arrangement. Choose beads that complement your arrangement's palette and style, whether it's the elegance of pearls or the vibrancy of gemstones.

Feathers

Incorporate feathers that resonate with your theme, whether it's the boldness of peacock feathers or the subtlety of downy plumes. You'll be surprised at how well their graceful presence will infuse your Ikebana with a touch of whimsy and emotional fluidity, captivating the viewer's imagination.

Vintage Keys

Vintage keys possess an enigmatic allure, symbolizing hidden stories and unspoken emotions. Incorporate these keys into your Ikebana as a metaphor for unlocking sentiments within your arrangement.

Fabric Swatches

Infuse tactile elegance into your Ikebana by incorporating fabric swatches. Tuck these delicate pieces of fabric around the vase or artfully drape them across the arrangement. Choose fabrics that harmonize with your arrangement's color palette and theme.

Small Mirrors

Small mirrors introduce a touch of magic to your Ikebana arrangements by creating reflections that amplify emotional depth. As viewers peer into these reflective surfaces, they become a part of the emotional journey, engaging with their own reflections as they connect with your arrangement's feelings.

Tiny Lanterns or Candles

For a touch of romance and warmth, incorporate tiny lanterns or candles into your Ikebana design. Whether they're nestled among the flowers or placed beside the vase, the gentle illumination casts a warm embrace around your arrangement.

Fragrant Elements

Incorporate fragrant elements such as dried herbs, lavender, or scented petals to engage another sensory dimension.

Calligraphy or Quotes

Introduce the art of calligraphy or carefully chosen quotes into your Ikebana designs. Place them on small cards, attached to stems, or within the vase itself.

Miniature Figurines

Tiny figurines, like a pair of lovebirds or a symbol of tranquility, can serve as symbolic representations of emotions within your Ikebana.

Draped Fabrics

Draped fabrics can introduce a soft and flowing element to your Ikebana, evoking feelings of comfort and tenderness. Allow a piece of sheer fabric to gently drape over the vase or cascade down the arrangement's side.

Personal Artifacts

Incorporate personal artifacts—a piece of jewelry, a keychain, or a small keepsake—that hold sentimental value. You can use personal artifacts to enrich your Ikebana with memories and stories that resonate on a deeply personal level.

Vintage Photographs

You can always integrate vintage photographs that hold sentimental value into your Ikebana arrangements to spice up your arrangement.

Unconventional Containers

Think beyond traditional vases and consider repurposing unconventional containers like teacups, vintage teapots, or heirloom bowls.

Scented Candles

Incorporate scented candles that complement the emotions you're conveying through your Ikebana. As the candlelight dances and the fragrance envelops the space, it creates an intimate ambiance that resonates with the feelings you've carefully curated within your arrangement.

Miniature Sculptures

Choose delicate miniature sculptures that align with the theme or emotions of your Ikebana.

Personal Letters or Notes

Include personal letters or handwritten notes within your Ikebana designs. These intimate messages can be placed discreetly among the flowers or tucked beneath the vase.

Seasonal Ikebana

In the ever-changing tapestry of nature, Ikebana finds its muse—the seasons that paint the world with their distinct hues and moods. Your arrangements, when tailored to fit different seasons, can mesmerize viewers and make them see the beauty that unfolds with the turning of time.

Imagine a picturesque garden that evolves with the dance of seasons. In the spring, delicate cherry blossoms blush the landscape with their soft pinks and whites. As summer approaches, vibrant sunflowers stretch towards the sky, basking in the golden warmth. When autumn arrives, fiery red maple leaves carpet the ground, creating a breathtaking display of nature's palette. And in the winter, snowflakes delicately dust the world, transforming it into a tranquil wonderland.

Within the changing seasons lies the heart of Ikebana's beauty—a celebration of impermanence and the fleeting moments that shape our lives. With every arrangement, you have the opportunity to capture the essence of each season, infusing your art with the spirit of nature's eternal rhythm.

Spring Ikebana

Spring, the season of hope and renewal!

Imagine yourself stepping into a blooming orchard, where cherry blossoms gently sway in the breeze, and the air is filled with their delicate fragrance. As an Ikebana artist, your art can capture this fleeting beauty and transform it into everlasting art by mastering the following Spring Ikebana tips:

Embrace the Blossoms

The cherry blossoms beckon you with their ethereal charm. As you gather them in your hands during Spring, you can notice how their delicate petals feel against your fingertips, soft and velvety. So, let the emotions of spring fill your heart, and with every arrangement, allow your passion for Ikebana to blossom just like these tender flowers.

Incorporate the art of space and asymmetry into your creations, letting each stem breathe and dance with its companions. Embrace the concept of *ma*, the space between elements, as it infuses your arrangements with a sense of serenity and balance. Let your Ikebana resonate with the rhythm of nature, creating arrangements that reflect the harmony of the universe.

Vibrant Tulips, Joyful Curves

Tulips stand tall and vibrant, displaying a kaleidoscope of colors that rival even the most brilliant of rainbows. As you select tulips for your arrangements, allow their joyful curves to guide your artistic vision. Blend different colors, and experiment with various tulip varieties, allowing each arrangement to become a unique expression of your creativity.

Play with height and movement, creating arrangements that seem to sway with the enthusiasm of a spring breeze. Remember, your Ikebana art isn't bound by rules but thrives on your emotions and imagination. Let the tulips take center stage, each bloom a brushstroke in the masterpiece that is your spring Ikebana.

Daffodils

Daffodils emerge from the earth like rays of sunshine, their bright blooms symbolizing the triumph of life over winter's cold embrace. Consider this as you work with daffodils and let their vibrant energy infuse your arrangements with the spirit of new beginnings. Embrace their sunny disposition and allow them to dance freely among other flowers and foliage.

Use contrasting textures and heights to create drama and depth, just as daffodils stand tall amidst the grass, boldly announcing the arrival of spring. As an artist, you can create arrangements that evoke emotions and tell stories. So, let the daffodils be your storytellers, whispering tales of warmth and hope in your spring Ikebana.

Beyond Traditional Vases

Spring Ikebana isn't confined to traditional vases alone. Embrace the spirit of innovation and let your creativity soar beyond the usual boundaries. Explore the art of incorporating Ikebana into unexpected places - perhaps a blooming branch on your bedroom wall, or a charming arrangement adorning your kitchen windowsill.

The magic of spring can manifest in the smallest of spaces, bringing joy and inspiration to your everyday life. Consider arranging a mini Ikebana on your desk, infusing your workspace with the freshness and optimism of the season. The possibilities are endless, and the world becomes your canvas for Ikebana expression.

Capture Fragility

Close your eyes and imagine strolling under a canopy of cherry blossoms in full bloom. The air is tinged with the delicate scent of these ethereal flowers, and a sense of awe washes over you. DurririnSpring Ikebana, you hold the power to capture this ephemeral beauty and turn it into everlasting art. Just like cherry blossoms, life is fleeting, and as you delicately arrange these tender blooms in a vase, feel the fragility of each petal against your fingertips.

Welcome the emotions that arise and let your heart's deepest longing for beauty and impermanence be awakened. As you craft your Ikebana, you become a storyteller, and each arrangement becomes a poem that celebrates the transient nature of life.

Embrace the Harmony of Contrasts

In Spring Ikebana, you witness the harmonious dance of contrasts, mirroring the complexities of life. As you work with the elegant tulips, you are reminded of the beauty in vulnerability and the strength that comes from bending but not breaking. Embrace the power of balance, as the softness of the daffodils finds equilibrium with the bold foliage.

Spring Ikebana Flower Arrangements to Inspire You

These captivating spring Ikebana flower arrangements capture the essence of the season's renewal and blooming beauty.

A. For blooming tranquility, you can experiment with these flowers:
- Cherry blossoms symbolize fleeting beauty and renewal.
- Peach blossoms represent longevity and vitality.
- Tulips evoke the spirit of spring with vibrant colors.
- Forsythia branches add a burst of yellow for a sunny touch.
- Lily of the Valley infuses a delicate fragrance and elegance.
- Baby's breath provides a soft, airy texture as an accent.

B. If you want your opting for a joyful and energetic creation, include any or all of these flowers:
- Daffodils radiate joyful energy and new beginnings.
- Hyacinths offer a rich scent and vibrant hues.
- Ranunculus brings layers of delicate petals in various colors.
- Grape hyacinths create a playful contrast with their small clusters.
- Freesias add elegance and a sweet fragrance.
- Foliage with Ferns provides a lush backdrop reminiscent of spring meadows.

C. Spring's wildflower fields also invoke joy to its beholders. If you're aiming for this type of vibe, try out the following:

- Cornflowers: Eliciting the charm of wildflower meadows.
- Queen Anne's Lace creates an intricate and lacy texture.
- Snapdragons adds height and vertical interest.
- Ranunculus brings a splash of color and vivaciousness.
- Solidago offers bursts of bright yellow, reminiscent of the sun.

D. If you're aiming for an arrangement that communicates serenity, you can include the following flowers in your arrangements:

- Narcissus embodies rebirth and self-discovery.
- Anemones infuse pops of color with delicate petals.
- Ranunculus offers a harmonious blend of form and texture.
- Viburnum adds a touch of greenery and a gentle fragrance.
- Muscari (Grape Hyacinths) create a whimsical and graceful touch.

E. For vibrant cherry blossom elegance, you can try:

- Cherry blossoms steal the show with their iconic and delicate blooms.
- Dogwood branches complement the cherry blossoms with their own charm.
- Peonies add luxurious layers of petals and sweet fragrance.
- Snowball viburnum evokes the feeling of a spring garden in full bloom.
- Sweet peas introduce a soft and romantic touch.

F. To capture the essence of Spring's whimsical breeze, experiment with:
- Pansies embrace the whimsy of spring with their colorful faces.
- Lilacs fill the arrangement with their exquisite scent and hues.
- Tulips create a vibrant focal point in various shades.
- Bleeding hearts offer a unique shape and symbolic meaning.
- Lily grass adds height and a sense of movement.

G. What's Spring without a fresh floral cascade feel? If you want to communicate freshness, add these flowers to your design.
- Cherry blossoms symbolize the fleeting nature of beauty and life.
- Tulips infuse a burst of color and vibrancy.
- Iris adds elegance and depth with their unique shape.
- Muscari (Grape Hyacinths) creates a whimsical touch with their clusters.
- Lily Grass introduces movement and a sense of flow to the arrangement.

H. If you're looking forward to Spring's warm and sun-like elements, give these flowers a go:
- Sunflowers evoke the warmth and energy of the sun.
- Ranunculus brings a burst of color and layers of petals.
- Daisies add a touch of simplicity and cheerfulness.

- Buttercups introduce delicate and vibrant blooms.
- Bupleurum provide a delicate touch of greenery.
- Peonies offer opulent and layered blooms in pastel shades.
- Lilacs fill the arrangement with their enchanting fragrance.
- Sweet Peas introduces soft and romantic petals in delicate hues.
- Baby's Breath adds an airy and ethereal touch.
- Eucalyptus provides a calming and aromatic element.

I. To communicate Spring's delicate whisper, you can play with these flowers in your Ikebana:
- Lily of the Valley infuses elegance and delicate fragrance.
- Bleeding hearts add a touch of romance and symbolism.
- Forget-Me-Nots evoke feelings of nostalgia and memory.
- Bellflowers introduce graceful and cascading blooms.
- Alchemilla (Lady's Mantle) provides gentle greenery and a soft texture.

Summer Ikebana: Warmth and Vitality

Step into the radiant world of Summer Ikebana, where nature's vibrant colors come alive, and the warmth of the sun's embrace is felt. Enchanted by the energy and vitality that surround you, the art of Summer Ikebana beckons, waiting to be explored.

Below are tips that can help you create the perfect Ikebana for Summer

The Majesty of Sunflowers: A Golden Ode to Sunshine

Imagine yourself amidst a golden sea of sunflowers, their radiant faces reflecting the sun's brilliance, and their energy coursing through your veins. Whispers of hope and happiness emanate from each sunflower, inviting you to celebrate life's grandeur.

As your hands arrange them in your Ikebana, their environment will be filled with an irresistible warmth, as different sunflower varieties are mixed, and their colors dance like a breathtaking painting of summer's allure. With sunflowers as your artistic companions, a vibrant celebration of life's abundance and endless possibilities is born in your Summer Ikebana.

Zinnias

If there was such a thing as a summer fiesta for flowers, zinnias would lead with their playful dance of colors, laughter and music filling the air. Bursting with vibrant hues, they will sing in harmony with the carefree spirit of the season.

Your creativity will flourish as zinnias are arranged in your Ikebana, pairing bright pinks with fiery oranges or mixing pastel zinnias with bold yellows to create a symphony of colors. You can mingle vivacious blooms and allow them to swirl. Doing this will evoke the joy and wonder of a summer's day.

With zinnias as your partners in the Summer, your Ikebana will always come alive, delighting with smiles and laughter.

Gladioli

As summer days stretch, the gladioli rise to exude elegance and strength. Like noble warriors, they stand tall and proud, reminding you of the resilience that resides within every human spirit. The drama and grandeur of these majestic blooms demand celebration.

Give the gladioli center stage in your summer arrangement and let their towering spikes reach upward. Also pair them with lush foliage that complements their elegance. You will be amazed at how much their presence would testify to the strength and sincerity that summer instills within us all. A sense of admiration for their beauty and the emotions they evoke will envelop you.

Again! Look Beyond the Vase

Beyond traditional vases, surprises await in Summer Ikebana. Picture a blooming branch adorning your bedroom wall, infusing your space with nature's embrace. A charming arrangement greets you each morning on your kitchen windowsill.

Use this image as an inspiration to embrace the idea of having a mini Ikebana vase on your desk. Watch how much this creative instinct will ignite your emotions and how this arrangement will spark joy in unexpected places. Implementing this tip will serve as a delightful oasis amidst a bustling workday during the summer. Your Summer Ikebana will become an artistic expression, turning the ordinary into the extraordinary.

Summer Ikebana Flower Arrangements to Inspire You

The goal of your Summer Ikebana should be to combine the warmth of the sun and the vibrant colors of nature to create stunning displays of emotion and beauty. So, experiment with the following summer Ikebana arrangements that encapsulate the spirit of the season:

    A. Tropical Elegance

Nature already shows us Summer's tropical elegance and you can be inspired by these floral options:
- Bird of Paradise evokes the exotic allure of tropical destinations.
- Hibiscus infuses vibrant colors and a touch of elegance.
- Orchids add a sense of luxury and delicate beauty.
- Monstera Leaves provide a lush and dynamic backdrop.
- Palm Fronds introduces height and a sense of movement.

B. Sunset Splendor

There's no Summer without some sunset splendor, and these flowers give you all the evening vibes you intend to achieve:
- Roses capture the warm hues of a summer sunset.
- Dahlias offer large and colorful blooms in various shades.
- Sunflowers embrace the radiant energy of the sun.
- Marigolds add a burst of orange and a touch of tradition.
- Zinnias provides a playful and joyful touch of color.

C. Coastal Serenity

For Summer's coastal serenity, these flowers will do all the communication:
- Sea Holly mimics the texture and beauty of coastal plants.
- Blue Delphinium elicits the feeling of the endless sky.
- Eryngium adds a touch of intrigue and spiky texture.
- Beach Grass creates a sense of movement and tranquility.
- Nigella (Love-in-a-Mist) infuses a delicate touch and subtle charm.

D. Garden Elegance

For a vibrant Summer Garden, go for these flowers:
- Lilies fill the arrangement with elegance and fragrance.
- Coneflowers evoke the wild beauty of summer gardens.
- Gladiolus adds vertical height and dramatic blooms.
- Snapdragons introduce a mix of colors and vertical interest.
- Queen Anne's Lace creates. a lacy and delicate backdrop.

E. Citrus Infusion

You may want to add a touch of citrus delight to your arrangement. These flowers are the perfect options to it:
- Gerbera Daisies offers a splash of color and cheerful energy.
- Calendula brings the vibrant shades of summer blooms.
- Lemon Leaves infuse a zesty and fresh aroma.
- Orange Ranunculus adds a pop of citrus-inspired color.
- Alstroemeria: Providing delicate blooms with a touch of contrast.

F. Blissful Symphony

We all look forward to Summer's bliss, and these flowers can evoke this vibe in your Ikebana:

- Daisies elicit the feeling of carefree summer days.
- Black-Eyed Susans mimic the beauty of wildflowers.
- Coreopsis adds vibrant pops of yellow and red.
- Achillea (Yarrow) creates a delicate and textured backdrop.
- Cosmos infuses an airy and whimsical touch.

G. Garden Oasis
If you're thinking about evoking a quiet, peaceful emotion on your beholders, try out the following:

- Hydrangeas offer lush and abundant blooms in various hues.
- Lavender adds fragrance and a sense of tranquility.
- Nigella (Love-in-a-Mist) introduces delicate blue blooms.
- Ferns provide a lush and natural backdrop.
- Baby's Breath creates an airy and ethereal touch.

I. Solstice Radiance
You can use these flowers to achieve Summer's solstice radiance:
- Sunflowers embody the energy and brightness of summer.
- Echinacea (Coneflowers) offer bold and vibrant petals.
- Cosmos adds delicate blooms and a playful touch.
- Daisies bring a sense of simplicity and cheerfulness.
- Statice provides texture and pops of color.

J. Garden Whimsy
For a garden whimsy Summer vibe, try these options:
- Sweet peas elicit the romance and fragrance of hidden gardens.
- Morning glories evoke the beauty of climbing vines.
- Nasturtiums add vibrant and edible blossoms.
- Ferns create a lush and verdant backdrop.
- Bells of Ireland infuses height and a touch of intrigue.

K. Coastal Dreamscape
You will be glad you added these flowers to your design:

- Blue Hydrangeas captures the serenity of coastal landscapes.
- Sea Lavender (Limonium) elicits the feeling of beachside blooms.
- Driftwood introduces a rustic and coastal element.
- Beach Grass creates a sense of movement and natural beauty.
- Baby's Breath provides an airy and delicate touch.

L. Summer Fiesta Joy
If you wish to communicate Summer's fiesta joy, these flowers are your go-to:
- Gerbera Daisies infuse vibrant colors and festive energy.
- Marigolds add a touch of tradition and warmth.
- Zinnias offer playful and cheerful blooms.

- Carnations create layers of texture and contrast.
- Delphiniums itroduces height and a sense of celebration.

M. Sunny Serenade
For a sunny serenade symphony, try these flowers:
- Sunflowers radiate the happiness and energy of summer.
- Coreopsis offer bursts of yellow and orange blooms.
- Daisies evoke the feeling of a sunny meadow.
- Snapdragons add vertical interest and a mix of hues.
Eucalyptus provides a fresh and aromatic touch.

Autumn Ikebana: Embrace the Warmth and Vivid Colors of the Season

Are you ready to witness nature's spectacular show of colors and dive headfirst into the magical world of Autumn Ikebana? Picture yourself amidst a breathtaking forest, where trees are adorned with leaves that are practically on fire – radiant reds, glowing golds, and warm oranges dancing in the sunlight. It's like stepping into an autumn wonderland!

Autumn Ikebana is all about capturing the essence of the season's warmth and beauty. But here's the best part: your Autumn Ikebana is not just an ordinary arrangement – it's a heartfelt expression of the season's emotions! Embrace the cozy and nostalgic vibes that autumn brings and let your heart guide your hands.

Allow each arrangement to become a tribute to the changing seasons, a beautiful way to celebrate nature's grand finale before the winter's rest.

Here are a few tips to inspire your Autumn Ikebana:

Chrysanthemums for the Win

Let's start by shining the spotlight on chrysanthemums – these blooms are like rays of sunshine, spreading their cheerful energy wherever they go. Get a hold of these happy beauties and let the joy seep into your Ikebana arrangements. Mix and match them with other autumn treasures like sunflowers and ornamental grasses, and let your creativity run wild!

Ginkgo Trees

Speaking of treasures, have you ever wandered under a canopy of ginkgo trees? Their fan-shaped leaves create a breathtaking golden carpet on the ground. We can't get enough of ginkgo leaves in Autumn Ikebana! They add an elegant touch and a sense of sophistication to your arrangements. Get ready to take your Ikebana to a whole new level of beauty!

Embrace Accessories

Now, let's set the mood – because autumn evenings are simply enchanting. Time to add a touch of coziness to your Ikebana by introducing some candlelight or fairy lights. Imagine your arrangements basking in a warm, flickering glow, creating a dreamy and romantic ambiance. It's like having your very own autumn oasis at home!

Wait, there's more!

Whimsical Berries

We've got a treasure trove of whimsical berries just waiting to be added to your Ikebana masterpieces. Beautyberry, hypericum, rose hips – they're like little gems in nature's treasure chest! Tuck them here and there in your arrangements to surprise and delight the eye. It's like a whimsical treasure hunt, Ikebana-style!

Autumn Ikebana is all about embracing the vividness and warmth of the season. So go ahead, create arrangements that reflect the beauty of nature's farewell dance. Let your imagination run free and allow your arrangements to be a heartfelt celebration of autumn's charms.

Autumn Ikebana Flower Arrangements to Inspire You

Try your hands on these Autumn Ikebana arrangements to communicate the pleasant embrace of the season:

1. Incorporate sunflowers, orange chrysanthemums, and wheat stems to evoke the fall harvest.

2. Combine red maple leaves, deep burgundy dahlias, and delicate white cosmos for a striking contrast.

3. Arrange yellow ginkgo leaves, goldenrod, and small branches in a low vase for a calming composition.

4. Mix dried hydrangeas, bittersweet vines, and dried corn husks for a cozy, rustic arrangement.

5. Use orange Asiatic lilies, red berries, and eucalyptus leaves to mimic the colors of a fall sunset.

6. Combine pinecones, acorns, ferns, and moss for an Ikebana that mirrors the beauty of the forest.

7. To leave your viewers fading into autumn, incorporate fading blooms like dahlias and roses alongside changing leaves for a transitioning arrangement

8. If you want to communicate warmth in Autumn, combine maroon ranunculus, orange gerbera daisies, and burgundy Japanese maple leaves for a harmonious display.

9. For a festival of fall colors, use a mix of vibrant flowers like orange marigolds, purple asters, and yellow chrysanthemums for a celebratory Ikebana.

Winter Ikebana: Embracing the Tranquility of the Season

Winter is a season where nature's stillness and serenity beckon you to create arrangements that reflect the quiet beauty of the season. As winter blankets the world in its icy embrace, the art of Winter Ikebana offers a canvas for your creativity to flourish, infusing your arrangements with a sense of calm and contemplation.

The Poetry of Evergreens: Timeless Elegance

Imagine yourself amidst a peaceful winter forest, the evergreens standing tall and steadfast, their branches dusted with snow like a magical fairytale. In Winter Ikebana, evergreens become the heart of your artistry, embodying resilience and life's continuity even in the coldest of seasons.

As you gather pine, cedar, or spruce branches, feel the strength and elegance they exude. Allow your arrangements to celebrate the majesty of evergreens, incorporating different varieties and textures to create a harmonious symphony of nature's grace. With evergreens as your muse, your Winter Ikebana becomes a timeless ode to the beauty of winter's embrace.

Winter Berries are Vibrant Jewels in the Snow

While winter may seem monochromatic, nature has hidden surprises to share. Picture stumbling upon a bush adorned with clusters of vibrant red berries, like jewels shining in the snow. These winter berries add a touch of vibrancy and life to your arrangements, igniting a spark of creativity in your heart.

Experiment with contrasting elements, pairing the fiery red of winter berries with the lush greens of evergreens. Let them dance together in your Ikebana, evoking the beauty of winter's dual nature - a season of tranquility and hidden vitality. With winter berries as your companions, your Winter Ikebana will become a vibrant celebration of life amidst the winter landscape.

Embrace Winter Blooms

As winter wraps the world in its icy shroud, a few brave flowers always dare to bloom, defying the chill with their delicate beauty. Blooms like camellias, hellebores, or even snowdrops naturally embody the spirit of endurance, reminding us that even in the harshest of times, beauty can thrive.

Create arrangements that reflect the ephemeral nature of these winter blooms, and allow them to shine like stars amidst the winter's cold canvas. Use contrasting textures and heights to evoke the drama and depth of winter's charm. Embrace the emotions that arise as you work with these blooms and let them whisper tales of hope and resilience in your Winter Ikebana.

Winter's Icy Splendor: Capture Nature's Magic

The magic of winter will reveal itself through frost and ice, paint delicate patterns on leaves and branches, and turn the world into a glistening wonderland. Embrace this phenomenon by adding elements like icy branches, dried seed pods, or even crystal accents to your design.

As you arrange these frosty elements, imagine the mesmerizing beauty of winter's radiance. Play with reflective surfaces and natural light, enhancing the magical glow of your Ikebana. The transformation that comes as light dances upon the frozen elements will turn your arrangement into an ethereal masterpiece that captures the essence of winter's enchantment.

Winter Ikebana Flower Arrangements to Inspire You

Winter Ikebana flower should capture the crispness of the air and the serene beauty of the season, and these captivating arrangements encapsulate the essence of the season:

      A. Frosty Elegance Wonderland
Everything appears white in winter, so why not try out these flowers?

- White roses symbolize purity and the pristine beauty of winter.
- Snowberries embody the charm of snow-covered branches.

- Dusty miller adds a touch of silvery foliage and texture.
- Pine cones introduce natural elements from the winter landscape.
- Eucalyptus provides a subtle fragrance and a fresh touch.

B. Enchanted Winter Forest

For a forest-esque Winter aesthetic, these are the best flowers to combine:
- Pine branches capture the majesty and strength of evergreens.
- White carnations offer a touch of snow-like elegance.
- Cedar twigs provide a rustic and aromatic backdrop.
- Red berries elicit the festive spirit and warmth of winter.
- Ilex (Holly) adds a traditional touch and a dash of color.

C. Icy Whispers Symphony

What's winter without ice? These flowers form the perfect camaraderie with snow:

- White lilies evokes a sense of purity and tranquility.
- Baby's breath creates a delicate and airy texture.
- Pine needle introduce a natural and fragrant element.
- Eryngium mimics frost-covered blooms with spiky elegance.
- Silver Brunia adds a touch of metallic sheen and modernity.

D. Silent Night Elegance

If you want flowers that complement the elements of Christmas, these are your top picks:
- Orchids offer a touch of sophistication and exotic beauty.
- Anemones elicit the ethereal charm of delicate winter flowers.
- Silver brunia adds a silvery sheen and unique texture.
- Dusty miiller creates a frosted and timeless backdrop.
- Eucalyptus pods introduce a rustic touch and fragrance.

E. Winter Moonlit Serenity

Winter is, without a doubt, the season that best communicates calm, and these flowers have all the elements of serenity:

- Calla lilies captures the elegance and grace of winter's simplicity.
- Pine cones introduce natural elements for an organic feel.
- Ranunculus offers layers of petals in soft and muted hues.
- Waxflowers create a delicate and ethereal touch.
- Baby's Breath infuses an airy and dreamlike quality.

F. Frozen Reflections Harmony

The winter breeze will only feel better with these flowers in sight:

Blue Hydrangeas elicits the cool tones and serenity of winter.
- White Tulips embody the purity and renewal of the season.
- Pine Needles create a natural and textured backdrop.

- Silver Brunia adds a touch of metallic shimmer.
- Eucalyptus introduces a fresh and aromatic element.

G. Cozy Fireplace Embrace

To enhance coziness winter? It only feels right to play around these flowers:
- Red Roses elicit warmth and the spirit of the holiday season.
- Hypericum berries add pops of red and festive charm.
- Cedar branches infuse a rustic and aromatic touch.
- Eucalyptus provides a fresh and calming element.
- Pine cones introduce a natural and festive accent.

H. Winter Frost Whispers

These flowers blend well with the frosty season:
- White Anemones mimic delicate snowflakes with their petals.
- Dusty Miller adds a silvery touch and texture.
- Silver Brunia creates a metallic and modern element.
- Eucalyptus infuses a fresh and aromatic backdrop.
- Pine needles introduces natural elements for a wintery feel.

I. Snowflake Serenade

For a sweet Winter serenade feel, thoughtfully marry these beautiful flowers together:
- White chrysanthemums elicit the charm of snow-covered blossoms.
- Lisianthus offers layers of delicate petals in white and soft hues.
- Hypericum berries add pops of red for contrast and warmth.
- Pine cones introduce natural elements from the winter landscape.
- Cedar twigs create a rustic and aromatic backdrop.

J. Winter Wonderland Dream

Combine these flowers to communicate a dreamland experience to yourself and everyone around you:
- Hydrangeas captures the cool and serene tones of winter.
- Dusty Miller adds a silvery touch and frosted texture.
- Silver Brunia creates a metallic and contemporary element.
- Pine Cones introduces natural elements for an organic feel.
- Eucalyptus infuses a fresh and calming fragrance.

General Seasonal Ikebana Tips: Unleash Your Artistic Magic with Nature's Beauty

Stay Prepared

Be ready to dive into the colorful world of Seasonal Ikebana! It's like a magical journey where you'll create masterpieces inspired by the beauty of nature and the ever-changing seasons, so you have got to have all the tool kits you need available.

Let Nature Be Your BFF

Who needs a rulebook when you've got Mother Nature on your side? Let the seasons be your mentors, and let nature's textures, colors, and vibes guide your Ikebana creations!

Incorporate Flowers that Sizzle

What's your favorite season? Sunflowers in summer? Cherry blossoms in spring? Chrysanthemums in autumn? Snowdrops in winter? The choice is yours, and each bloom sings its own seasonal song! So, feel free to pick the flowers that best encapsulate the season.

Don't Be Scared to Mix Elements

Don't shy away from playing with textures like an artistic DJ! Mix and match smooth evergreen needles with wild and untamed dried seed pods. Your arrangements will be a tactile masterpiece!

Let Colors Pop Like Fireworks

Make your Ikebana sizzle with colors! From bold and bright in summer to warm and cozy in autumn, your arrangements will be a kaleidoscope of nature's best hues when you incorporate the right colors.

Asymmetry Is Good!

Dear artist, the temptation to create the perfect Ikebana comes to us all. However, forget perfection and embrace the beauty of asymmetry! Your Ikebana will groove like a jazz band as each stem finds its rhythm in a harmonious dance!

Make Space for Zen

The magic of *Ma* is your secret weapon! Use it and thank *Ma* later. Don't overcrowd your arrangements; let your blooms breathe and enjoy the Zen vibes of negative space!

Feel the Ikebana Emotion

Your arrangements should speak louder than words! So, feel the joy of spring, the excitement of summer, the coziness of autumn, and the calm of winter in every petal and incorporate these emotions into your design.

Sniff and Smile
What's that delightful fragrance? Oh, it's your Ikebana arrangements! By adding scented flowers like lilacs in spring and roses in summer, you'll awaken so many olfactory lobes!

Celebrate Ikebana Style
Ikebana isn't just an art; it's a celebration! Add festive elements that scream, "It's spring! It's summer! It's autumn! It's winter!" Your arrangements will party like there's no tomorrow!

Let Your Ikebana Spirit Soar
Again, always remind yourself that you are the Ikebana magician! Embrace the journey, celebrate your uniqueness, and let your Ikebana arrangements be an expression of your blooming soul!

CHAPTER 5

Creating Your Own Ikebana Arrangements

By stepping into this chapter, you're embarking on a journey of self-expression and artistic discovery. So, get ready to feel the thrill of planning and preparing, Immerse yourself in the step-by-step instructions and be guided by the wisdom of centuries-old techniques.

You will also learn about challenges and how to avoid or overcome them. All the inspiration you need from diverse sources are embedded in this chapter, including century-old techniques on how to start your own Ikebana designs and make them stand out.

Planning and Preparation

You must ensure to be meticulous from the get-go to achieve the best results.

Here are important planning tips to help you bring your creative ideas to life:

Create the Right Atmosphere for Your Vision

Start by carving out a dedicated workspace that becomes a cocoon of inspiration. When considering your options, ensure to choose an area bathed in natural light, free from disruptions. Arrange your tools and materials within easy reach, so that you can create an immersive space that invites you to explore the artistry of Ikebana.

Equip Yourself with the Right Tools

Gather your tools, each a vital instrument in sculpting your Ikebana masterpiece. Pick up your pruning shears: they are your silent allies in precision cutting. Ensure that they are properly sharpened.

Don't forget your floral wire and Kenzan too. These tools aren't just objects; they are extensions of your artistic vision, waiting to breathe life into your arrangement.

Select Flowers and Foliage

Choose the flowers and foliage you'll need to create your vision. As you select your elements, think beyond their visual appeal.

Pair flowers that complement each other. For example, you can pair the vibrant daisies with the elegant curve of calla lilies because the combination of these two flowers can craft a juxtaposition of playfulness and sophistication within your arrangement.

Just ensure to be thoughtful and intentional when selecting your materials.

Prepare Your Workspace

Arrange your tools with purpose, ensuring they're at your fingertips. Secure the kenzan firmly within your chosen container. Thoughtfully position your materials, allowing each stem to harmonize with the others. Set up your water vessel nearby. Having everything in place before you begin minimizes interruptions.

Trim and Condition Your Flowers

Trimming and conditioning your flowers is pivotal in Ikebana because it helps your flowers stay in shape. Trim stems at angles with care and remove any leaves that will be submerged in water to prevent decay. Conditioning your materials ensures their freshness.

Visualize Your Creation

What do you want your flowers to look like after arranging them? This is one question you must settle in your heart from the beginning of your creation. Before embarking on the tangible arrangement, close your eyes and mentally unfold your composition. Picture the graceful curve of branches, the delicate flutter of petals, and the interplay of colors.

Set the Right Foundation

The final stage in preparation involves setting the right foundation for your arrangement. Place heavy, base materials like taller stems and thick branches in the kenzan to establish balance and stability. Then proceed to add your primary and secondary materials to bring your design to life.

Step-by-Step Instructions

Let's proceed to unlock the secrets to creating breathtaking arrangements that evoke emotion and grace. Those creative thoughts in your head can be brought to light if you follow the right tips, all of which have been laid down in this chapter.

Use all the steps judiciously and you will realize how much of a genius you are:

Step 1: Preparation

Much has been discussed already about preparing for your Ikebana, but here's a few more tips you could find useful.

Make sure you tick the following boxes before proceeding to the next step:

1) Determine where you want to work: remember to choose a spot with considerable light.
2) Have the right tools at hand. Here are the basic things you'll need:
   - Pruning Shears: To trim stems with precision.
   - Floral Wire: Useful for securing delicate elements.
   - Kenzan (Frog): A spiked holder to anchor stems in place.
   - Water Vessel: Choose a container that complements your arrangement.
   - Candle: Not necessary if you don't want them, but candles can come in handy, especially at night.
   - Music: As an addendum, you can play your favorite tunes to create a calming ambiance.

Step 2: Arrangement

With preparation now in the bag, the next thing to do is arrange your flowers the way you want them to appear. Ensure to take note of the following:

Observe Balance and Symmetry

As you arrange, pay attention to balance and symmetry. Distribute visual weight evenly across the arrangement. Experiment with height, color, and form to create a harmonious composition.

Incorporate *Ma* to Your Arrangement

Embrace the concept of *Ma* by leaving room for empty spaces to add depth and visual interest. These spaces invite the viewer's eye to explore and appreciate the arrangement. Remember to also incorporate gentle curves and angles to introduce movement.

Step Back and Assess Your Arrangement

One thing I love to do is step back and assess how far I have gone with my design and how well I am progressing. This helps me to identify errors quickly and make corrections. If you're going to achieve an impeccable design, you must also do the same.

Consider whether the arrangement aligns with your initial vision and make any necessary adjustments to achieve the desired aesthetic.

Consider the Environment

Take your environment into account when arranging your flowers. Since different flowers thrive in different conditions, ensure your arrangement is well-suited to its surroundings. Factors like the temperature and humidity of your workspace should be thoroughly scrutinized. Your flowers will only thrive when you create the perfect environment for them.

Create a Focal Point

Designate a focal point in your arrangement. Choose one element that stands out and draws the viewer's attention and build your arrangement from that standpoint. Of course, you must have ensured that your primary and secondary elements complement each other during the preparation step.

Texture and Contrast

Do you recall all that was discussed about contrast in Chapter 4? Now is the time to put it to good use.

Incorporate texture and contrast into your design to create visual intrigue. For instance, you can mix soft petals with spiky foliage or delicate blooms with sturdy stems. These elements, although distinct, blend perfectly when combined to form a visual masterpiece.

Grouping and Clustering

Plan to group similar elements together to create clusters. You can experiment with different groupings to find the most appealing arrangement.

Expressive Lines
Pay attention to the lines created by your stems and elements. Utilize slanting lines, vertical lines, and curves to guide the viewer's eye and evoke specific emotions.

Layering and Depth
Create layers within your arrangement to add depth. Place some elements closer to the viewer and others deeper within the arrangement.

Reflect on Proportions
Evaluate the proportions of your arrangement. Ensure that the height, width, and overall size are suitable for the container and the space it will inhabit.

Final Touches
Once satisfied with your arrangement, give it a final review. Tuck in any stray stems or adjust elements for optimal presentation. Ensure that the arrangement is stable and secure.

Water and Hydration
Fill your water vessel with clean water. Before placing your stems in the kenzan, dip them in water to ensure they're properly hydrated. Hydration prolongs the life of your arrangement.

The Final Gaze
Once you're satisfied with your arrangement, step away and give it a final gaze from different angles. Ensure that it looks appealing from all sides and angles, as it may be viewed from various perspectives.

Reflect and Appreciate Your Work
As you admire your Ikebana arrangement, appreciate the effort and creativity you've poured into each step.

Troubleshooting Tips

Like any other form of art, you'll encounter the twists and turns that come with arranging flowers creatively. However, this shouldn't make you afraid. Every challenge that arises simply becomes an opportunity to nurture the blossom of resilience within you.

Together, we shall unravel the secrets to overcoming obstacles and transforming them into stepping stones on the path to Ikebana mastery.

Wilting Woes

The heartache of witnessing your cherished blooms wither prematurely is a challenge that every Ikebana artist must face, but don't be afraid: there are ways to extend the life of your precious elements and keep them vibrant for longer.

One secret lies in giving them a fresh cut, akin to a rejuvenating spa treatment for flowers. Before arranging, immerse the stems in warm water and make a slanted cut to increase their water absorption. This simple act breathes new life into your flowers, allowing them to bloom and shine with renewed vigor.

Another trick to thwart wilting is to choose elements with varying stages of bloom. This clever strategy ensures that while some blooms may fade, others will continue to unfurl and add a touch of enchantment to your arrangement. Embrace the ebb and flow of life within your Ikebana, celebrating the beauty of each stage.

Balancing Act

The dance of asymmetry is a delightful aspect of Ikebana, but it can also be a challenging tightrope walk. Achieving that perfect balance between elements may seem like chasing fireflies in the dark, but don't be afraid because there is a foolproof method to master this artful tightrope.

Start by selecting a central focal point, a star that guides the arrangement's direction. Visualize an invisible line that extends from this focal point, creating a path along which the other elements will gracefully dance. As you add each stem, consider its weight, height, and overall presence, adjusting their positions along the imaginary line. Trust your intuition: it is the innate sense of harmony that will lead you to create arrangements that captivate the eye and the soul.

Space Odyssey

The enchantment of *Ma*, the space between elements, is what breathes life into Ikebana. However, finding that perfect balance of space can be an odyssey of its own. Too much space, and your arrangement may feel disconnected and disjointed; too little, and it becomes suffocating, stifling the essence of Ikebana's grace.

To master the art of *Ma*, tap into your emotions as you arrange the elements. Allow the space to embrace the story your arrangement wishes to tell, giving it room to breathe and speak its truth. As you observe the spaces between each stem, imagine them as moments of silence in a mesmerizing symphony, where each pause holds the promise of something yet to come. The dance of *Ma* is a gentle reminder that within the stillness, the magic of Ikebana unfurls its petals.

Structural Snags

The structural integrity of your Ikebana arrangement is the backbone that upholds its enchantment. Yet, building this foundation can pose a challenge as you navigate the artful interplay of strength and delicacy.

Begin by selecting sturdy materials as your base, forming a reliable structure that anchors the arrangement. Imagine it as the skeleton that supports the body of your creation. Once your foundation is set, weave in the delicate elements, like a dress of lace enveloping a powerful warrior. The key is to ensure that each element complements and reinforces the others, forming a harmonious dance of strength and grace.

Colors Collide

The kaleidoscope of colors that bloom in an Ikebana arrangement is one of its most captivating features. However, the collision of colors can also lead to a visual cacophony, disrupting the harmony you seek.

To tame this riot of colors, study and master the art of color psychology and symbolism. Make sure you find out the the emotions and meanings associated with each hue, as well as how they interact with one another. For example, a monochromatic arrangement can evoke a sense of serenity, while complementary colors can spark a lively energy.

Allow your intuition to guide you in selecting the colors that resonate with your heart and the story you wish to express.

Learn through Adaptation

The essence of Ikebana lies not only in its artistic beauty but also in its ability to embody the spirit of resilience. Always remember that adaptation is the hallmark of the Ikebana artist.

Embrace the imperfections that emerge, for they are the brushstrokes that paint the canvas of your growth. In every withered petal or misplaced stem, you find an opportunity to learn and evolve. Like a phoenix rising from the ashes, let each setback become a springboard to launch yourself to new heights of artistic prowess.

Through each trial, remind yourself that even nature's elements bend with the winds of change, and so shall you. Embrace the beauty that emerges from flexibility and find joy in the process of overcoming hurdles. As you face obstacles head-on, see them not as barriers but as invitations to elevate your artistry to new levels.

Inspiration and Resources

Nature's Embrace

At the heart of Ikebana lies an unbreakable bond with nature—an eternal dance between the artist and the elements. Seek inspiration in the world that surrounds you, where every tree, every meadow, and every gentle breeze tells a tale of beauty and grace.

Take leisurely strolls through parks, gardens, and woodlands, immersing yourself in the ever-changing scenery. Allow the rustling leaves and fragrant blooms to whisper their secrets to you, revealing the secrets of form and texture. The beauty of Ikebana is in its ability to capture these fleeting moments and immortalize them in an arrangement that speaks to the soul.

The Poetry of Art

Inspiration is not just limited to the realm of flora and fauna. Embrace the poetry of art in all its forms, from the classics to the avant-garde. Wander through art galleries and museums, absorbing the emotions conveyed by masterpieces on canvas or in stone.

With every brushstroke and chisel mark, you'll find a language that transcends words—a language that your Ikebana can echo. Feel the rhythm of colors, the interplay of light and shadow, and the emotions that emanate from each artwork. As you infuse these inspirations into your arrangements, your Ikebana becomes a living poetry of the human experience.

Cultural Treasures

Ikebana is a vessel of cultural heritage, passed down through generations like a precious family heirloom. Delve into the history and traditions of Ikebana, unearthing the stories that shape its essence.

Explore the wisdom of past masters, whose teachings resonate through the ages. Learn from their trials and triumphs, drawing upon their expertise to refine your own craft. As you discover the cultural tapestry woven into Ikebana, you'll find a deeper appreciation for this art form that transcends time and space.

Blooming Community

The journey of an Ikebana artist need not be a solitary one. Seek out fellow enthusiasts, forming a vibrant community that celebrates the beauty of floral artistry together.

Attend workshops and gatherings, where the exchange of ideas and techniques becomes a symphony of creativity. In the warmth of camaraderie, you'll find a wellspring of encouragement and inspiration. Cherish the friendships that bloom amidst shared passions, for within this community lies the nurturing soil where your artistic dreams can take root and flourish.

Ikebana Publications

Expand your horizons with contemporary interpretations and groundbreaking approaches to Ikebana. Engage with fellow enthusiasts through forums and social media, where ideas are shared, and connections are forged. The online realm serves as a gateway to endless possibilities, as you discover the works of artists from all corners of the world.

Floral Flair

Nature is abundant with surprises, and the world of floristry holds a treasure chest of possibilities. Attend floral exhibitions and shows, where blooms of every shape and hue bedazzle the senses.

Let the kaleidoscope of flowers spark your imagination, and draw inspiration from floral arrangements that transcend conventional norms. From elaborate installations to whimsical creations, the world of floristry offers a glimpse of what blooms in the realm of limitless creativity.

CHAPTER 6

THE IMPORTANCE OF IKEBANA

Ikebana Is a Reflection of Harmony and Balance

Harmony and balance are seen in Ikebena. It represents a blend of attributes that are in perfect equilibrium that that goes beyond geographical boundaries and cultural differences. Unlike the opulent extravagance often associated with Western floral arrangements, Ikebana's appeal springs from its exquisite restraint.

Each meticulously selected element within an Ikebana composition is not just a decorative component; it's a profound choice full of symbolism and intent, weaving together a breathtaking tapestry of form, space, and color that tantalizes the senses and evokes a rich display of emotions.

Ikebana is A Pilgrimage of the Soul

Ikebena is more than just an art form. Around the world, devoted practitioners and enlightened monks embarked on the profound journey of Ikebana over time, seeing it as a conduit for spiritual expression, a medium to communicate reverence and devotion through the meticulous arrangement of blossoms.

This creative journey transforms into a soulful pilgrimage that calls on practitioners to traverse the landscapes of impermanence. Just as petals unfold, grace the world, and gently return to the earth, Ikebana stands as a significant reminder of life's transient nature. In acknowledging this transience lies an invitation to also recognie the beauty of every moment and appreciation for it.

Ikebana teaches practitioners to find beauty in the transitory nature of life. Just as flowers bloom, wither, and gracefully fade away, Ikebana reminds us of the impermanence of all things. This understanding encourages us to embrace the fleeting moments and find beauty and meaning in the transient aspects of life, sparking a sense of reverence for the ebb and flow of existence.

Embracing Minimalism and Simplicity

In the midst of so much noise that is associated with modern existence, Ikebana emerges as a safe space, a sanctuary steeped in simplicity and mindfulness. By orchestrating an artful choreography of carefully selected elements, Ikebana introduces you to the beauty of simplicity and minimalism. Each blossom, leaf, and stem takes center stage, resonating with a unique narrative, pointing to whispers of individual stories told in a harmonious ensemble.

This minimalist ideology not only finds expression in the physical composition but also weaves into the very fabric of the arranger's mindset. Through the practice of Ikebana, clutter is shed, not just from the floral arrangement but from the corridors of life as well. You can free up your mind from bugging and nagging thoughts just by engaging in floral pattern arrangements.

Ikebana Is An Expression of the Seasons

Ikebana's seasonal narrative mirrors the symbiotic dance between nature's ebb and flow and the human experience.There is aocnnection between the season and the flowers, just like humans also go through differetn seasons and phases. Each season passes on its own treasury of blooms and greenery, each resonating with symbolic layers and creating a beautiful feeling.

With spring, Ikebana comes alive in a cascade of cherry blossoms and lively tulips, a representative of renewal and aspirations. Summer's Ikebana pulsates with vigor and fertiity, mirroring the earth's blossoming. In autumn, arrangements echo nature's transformation as leaves transform into gold and blossoms bow in graceful homage, inviting introspection and calm. Winter's Ikebana mirrors the hush of the season, employing bare branches and delicate blooms to show the appeal of serenity.

Ikebana Connects Artists From All Over the World

While Ikebana's roots are firmly embedded in Japanese culture, its influence extends far past the boundaries of Japan. In our interconnected world, Ikebana has entranced individuals hailing from diverse backgrounds. As a result, practitioners of Ikebana irrespective of where they come from can discover a common ardor and admiration for the elegance of nature.

So, it's no longer just about the Japanese. Ikebana unifies millions around the world from different places. It has become a focal point where interests align.

Ikebana is a Paradigm of Self Discovery

Engaging with Ikebana embarks you on a journey of self-discovery and creative expression. In the intricate choreography of arranging, the artist unveils pieces of their inner realm, intricately weaving stories and sentiments through the meticulous orchestration of each stem and bloom.

This purposeful practice within Ikebana serves as an instrument for nurturing mindfulness and abiding tranquility. Amid the dance of petals, you can harmonize with nature and discover yourself. You can come to a place of recognition of who yo are from the carefu selection of floral patterns. You can also come to a place of better understanding of your tendencies, moods and emotions with Ikebana.

Ikebana Is a Source of Joy and Inspiration

Ikebana's influence extends beyond the confines of meditation—it also becomes a reservoir of exuberance and inspiration. The very act of weaving flowers into harmonious ensembles yields a spark of elation, as creators begin to see their visions materialize. Each creation becomes a story, a memory, or a vignette from a transient moment. Consequently, every arrangement transforms into an inception of inspiration and marvel, bridging wonder between the artist and the observer.

Ikebana Is A symbol of Legacy and Renewal

As artists engage with Ikebana, they pay homage to a lineage of masters who have passed their skills and wisdom from generation to generation.

The tenets of Ikebana stems from an indelible tapestry, its threads woven by artists who honor their heritage. This dance between the age-old and the contemporary ensures Ikebana's tenacity—a living art form that seamlessly marries tradition and innovation, persisting as an everlasting testament to the passage of time.

Ikebana Cultivates Mindfulness and Connection

In a modern era characterized by incessant diversions and an overwhelming amount of information, Ikebana emerges as a haven of mindfulness. Within the ritual of crafting floral compositions, you can immerse yourself in solace within the act of floral patterns and arrangements.

Ikebana is a ground for growing your consciousnes of nature and its properties. It is a point of establishing a connection with your surroundings. Away from all the noise of life and its concerns.

As artisans meticulously elect and amalgamate each constituent, an intimate rapport forms with the resources they use. This rapport stretches forth to embrace the natural world in its fullness and leads to an appreciation for the way forms are intertwined and blended in perfect harmony.

Ikebana Is A Timeless and Ever-Evolving Art Form

Ikebana's ageless allure resides within its capacity to transcend through generations, steadfastly retaining its relevance within the contemporary period. Over centuries, it has evolved, while keeping its simple minmallistic form.

Ikebena has picked different attributes from the different eras it has been in existence. It has adapted to different times and seasons, and as such become a representation of evolution. It gives you a glimpse into the past of people who practiced the art centuries ago.

It is an art form that speaks of how mankind can evolve and change over time, and how it is possible to retain some aspects of life that are core to your existence.

Ikebana Is A Bridge Between Past and Future

Ikebena connects the past with the future. As we have seen that it is a relic of old times, it goes on to become a source of inspiration for modern day artists.

There is so much wisdom and technique that is transferred from Ikebena over time, and it eventually builds a bridge that connects the old with the new. This is one of the ey attributes of Ikebena. It takes from the new, and merges with the old, creating a unique art expression while yet retaining some critical components of the old techniques.

This way Ikebena is able to adapt to new trends, techniques and innovations, but still retain its minimalist and simplistic nature. Artists also get better because they are able to draw from the inspiration of centuries old patterns to create modern day patterns that still carry the same tenacity and expression.

Ikebana Is A Language of Beauty and Expression

Beyond words, Ikebana effortlessly communicates a language of beauty and epression. It gracefully surmounts the constraints of words and connects with the artist at a personal level. Each arrangement is an envoy of emotions, narratives, and sentiments that conventional language many times is incapable of communicating.

Ikebana has its own vocabulary and style of communication that can only be understood by those who appreciate nature and its diversities.

Ikebana Embraces Imperfection and Wabi-Sabi

Amid the ceaseless pursuit of flawlessness, the world often disregards the allure concealed within imperfections. Ikebana, with its focus on simplicity and equilibrium, the flawed and the transient. This ideology resonates profoundly with the essence of the Japanese aesthetic philosophy—wabi-sabi.

Wabi-sabi endorses the beauty that is inherent in imperfection, transience, and organic decline. Ikebana practitioners wholeheartedly embrace this philosophy, uncovering appeal within asymmetry, unorthodox configurations, and the ephemeral cadence of blossoms. Every arrangement mirrors the lifecycle, an intricate dance where magnificence resides not solely in the zenith of full bloom, but equally within the wilting petals and their graceful descent—an homage to the transient ephemerality encompassing all facets of existence.

Via wabi-sabi, Ikebana becomes a significant reminder of the fleeting nature of life. It rmeinds us that our time here is temporoary and we must make of it as much beauty as possible, so that we can look back at tend and still recognize beauty that was created along the way.

Ikebana Is A Sustainable Art Form

Ikebena places so much emphasis on simplicity and minimalism. In Ikebena, less is more. What this does is to encourage judicious stewardship of resources which is also important for keeping our planet. This artistic discipline encourages practitioners to contemplate their choice of blossoms and verdure, removing excess and unnecessary ostentation.

Every stem and foliage is important in ikebana, and must be accounted for. Ikebana asks, "Why are you using this? What is the intent of this pattern?"
Everything must have a meaning because in finding meaning, waste is prevented and the planet is preserved.
Ikebana tells us of the world around us and that it must be kept. In a time of global climate crisis, Ikebana reminds us that this earth should be safeguarded.

Ikebana Is A Path to Growth

Ikebana surpasses the realm of a mere pastime; it emerges as a passage to self-revelation and individual evolution. As you give yourself to the tapestry of flower arrangement, you delve deeper into areas of yourinnermost being you never thought were there. You can discover layers of emotions, apprehensions, and elations.

The act of creation many times ffunctions as a mirror, reflecting the patterns of your thoughts, sentiments, strengths, weaknesses, fears and joys. Ikebana has the ability to bring a person to a place of self-discovery. It establishes a bond with the soul of a person to a point where you can see yourself for all you really are.

The truth is that no artisna gets it right the first time. But as artisans progress on their Ikebana journey, they encounter trials and victories, culminating in personal growth and metamorphosis. Ikebena helps in self-discovery as new patterns are uncovered and tried. Patterns reflect a great deal of who we are, and what our choices have been over time. They also give us an idea of the possibilities that exist when we embrace newness, change and growth.

Ikebana Is A Source of Inspiration for Other Art Forms

The influence of Ikebana extends far beyond the confines of floral composition, permeating a multitude of art forms and diverse creative spheres.

In the realm of architecture, Ikebana has cast its profound influence upon the conception of negative space, guiding architects to sculpt spaces that give an aura of tranquility and peace. The integration of organic elements—whether it is the lush green of vegetation or the fluidity of water features—resonates deeply with Ikebana's intimate affiliation with the environment.

Within the domain of haute couture, Ikebana's exquisite form and aesthetics ignite the creative spark within designers, birthing ensembles that serve as mirrors to the art form's inherent elegance and understated grandeur. The concept and features of minimalism and the artful harnessing of negative space weave themselves seamlessly into the fabric of contemporary fashion, casting an echo of Ikebana's timeless allure onto the canvas of the modern era.

So you can see that it is all connected. Ikebena is not just about floral patterns. Indeed, it has deep roots that spread into language, medicine arhcitecture, photography, cinematography and of course poetry among others.

Even though it has a vocabulary of its own, Ikebana speaks to other art forms and gives them materials to transform. It gives ideas in its purest or crudest form so that artists can create. But it also has the ability to modify raw ideas into finished works. So whether it is at the beginning or the end, Ikebana serves as a source of inspiration.

CHAPTER 7
THE ROLE OF IKEBANA IN JAPANESE CULTURE

Ikebana has been an integral part of Japan's rich cultural heritage for centuries, influencing various aspects of Japanese life, spirituality, and aesthetics.

Aesthetic Expression

Rooted in historical court rituals during the Heian period, Ikebana's influence extends into modern Japan. Every design in Japan screams "Ikebana," from traditional architecture to modern day technological innovations.

Historically, Ikebana played a pivotal role in Japan's love for aesthetics. Notable events in Japan's Ikebana history include:

- A. **Heian Imperial Court Rituals:** During the Heian period, from 794 to 1185, Ikebana found its beginnings as an integral part of elaborate court rituals.

- B. **World War II and Ikebana's Resilience:** In the midst of World War II, Ikebana became a source of solace and creative expression for the Japanese people.

- C. **Ikebana's Post-War Revival:** After World War II, Ikebana underwent a revival as a part of Japan's recovery and cultural resurgence.

- D. **Global Spread and Contemporary Influence:** Over time, Ikebana transcended borders and gained international recognition.

Cultural Tradition

Originating as floral offerings during Buddhist ceremonies in the

Nara and Heian periods, Ikebana has seamlessly transitioned into the modern era, and as a cultural cornerstone, it continues to help the Japanese government promote cultural tourism, showcasing its rich history to the world in the following ways;

- A. **Cultural Tourism Attraction**: Ikebana's cultural significance serves as a captivating allure for tourists by immersing them in Japan's historical and artistic heritage.
- B. **Regional Engagement**: Government-backed Ikebana exhibitions and workshops across regions not only attract tourists but also engage local communities, bolstering their participation in preserving and sharing cultural traditions.
- C. **Economic Ripples**: Ikebana-centric tourism continues to generate a ripple effect for the economy of Japan by stimulating various sectors of the economy (hospitality, transportation, and more).

Meditative Practice

Ikebana's meditative approach invites practitioners to connect with nature on a profound level. Delicately placing each stem allows individuals to immerse themselves in a serene dance with the environment. With its roots in Zen Buddhism, Ikebana's therapeutic qualities have withstood the test of time.

Ikebana inspires meditative practices in Japan in the following ways:

- A. **Mindful Contemplation**: Ikebana's deliberate arrangement of flowers encourages practitioners to engage in mindful contemplation, fostering a sense of tranquility and connection with nature.
- B. **Therapeutic Escape:** Ikebana's rhythmic process offers a therapeutic escape from the fast-paced modern world, allowing individuals to find solace and rejuvenation in the act of arranging flowers.
- C. **Urban Retreat:** Ikebana provides a serene escape for individuals seeking a break from the urban chaos, nurturing a sense of calm amidst the hustle and bustle of bustling Japanese cities.

Teaching Discipline and Patience

Ikebana is a disciplined practice that requires meticulous attention to detail, echoing Japan's historical values of discipline and patience., and as a nurturing process, it instills patience and cultivates a deep appreciation for the subtleties of each stem.

Nowadays, these values of Ikebana can be evidently seen in different aspects of modern Japan such as:

- A. **Precision in Craftsmanship:** Ikebana's meticulous approach mirrors the precision found in traditional Japanese craftsmanship, such as woodworking and ceramics, where attention to detail is paramount.
- B. **Academic Excellence**: The discipline ingrained in Ikebana resonates in Japan's renowned education system, emphasizing hard work and dedication in achieving academic excellence.
- C. **Culinary Artistry:** Ikebana's patient and careful arrangement of elements parallels the meticulous preparation of Japanese cuisine, reflecting the nation's culinary dedication.
- D. **Corporate Culture:** Ikebana's attention to detail and patience reflects the values within Japan's corporate culture, where diligence, respect for processes, and collaborative efforts are valued.
- E. **Sports and Martial Arts:** The discipline practiced in Ikebana translates to Japan's tradition of martial arts and sports, where dedication and patience are key to achieving mastery.
- F. **Technological Precision:** Ikebana's emphasis on precision aligns with Japan's reputation for technological innovation, where attention to detail drives advancements in various fields.
- G. **Architectural Excellence**: Ikebana's meticulous approach finds echoes in Japan's architectural precision, where attention to detail and craftsmanship are evident in the nation's iconic buildings and structures.
- H. **Gardening Traditions:** Ikebana's patience and respect for natural elements are reflected in Japan's traditional gardening practices, showcasing a deep appreciation for nature's beauty.
- I. **Fashion Industry:** Ikebana's emphasis on detail and harmony influences Japan's fashion industry, seen in the careful curation of fabrics, patterns, and designs, reflecting the nation's fashion-forward reputation.
- J. **Educational Approach**: Ikebana's teaching of patience and discipline aligns with Japan's educational approach, where students are encouraged to invest time and effort to master subjects and skills.

Interior Decoration

Japanese love for subtle beauty and minimalism finds its roots in Ikebana. Historical examples of Ikebana's integration with architecture date back to the Azuchi-Momoyama period, where arrangements were thoughtfully selected to complement interior design.

The art of arranging flowers has not stopped influencing interior aesthetics in contemporary Japan as it continues to harmoniously merge the natural world with modern living environments.

Ceremonial Use

Japan's traditional ceremonies are laced with Ikebana symbolisms that infuse layers of meaning. The towering "Rikka" style, with its roots in the Momoyama period, symbolized the harmonious relationship between humanity and nature. Fast forward to today and these arrangements have continued to hold weight in Japanese cultural and religious ceremonies, reflecting Japan's cultural identity and values.

- A. **Tea Ceremony (Chado):** Ikebana arrangements contribute to the ambiance of the tea ceremony, reflecting harmony, respect, and the changing seasons.

- B. **Weddings (Kekkon):** Ikebana arrangements adorn wedding venues, symbolizing the couple's harmonious union and a life in bloom.

- C. **Funerals (Soshiki):** Ikebana holds a somber role in funeral rituals, representing the ephemeral nature of life and the passage of time.

- D. **Coming of Age (Seijin Shiki):** Ikebana decorations mark the transition to adulthood, signifying growth, beauty, and responsibility.

- E. **Children's Day (Kodomo no Hi):** Ikebana's presence during this celebration of children represents hope, strength, and a bright future.

- F. **Cherry Blossom Viewing (Hanami):** Ikebana's presence enhances the beauty of cherry blossom festivals, highlighting the fleeting nature of spring's splendor.

- G. **New Year (Oshogatsu):** Ikebana arrangements welcome the new year, symbolizing renewal, good fortune, and a fresh start.

H. **Shichi-Go-San (7-5-3 Festival):** Ikebana designs adorn the celebrations for children's growth and well-being, representing familial love and support.

I. **Buddhist Offerings (Ho-onko):** Ikebana arrangements are offered as symbols of respect and gratitude to ancestors during Buddhist memorial services.

J. **Temple Festivals (Matsuri):** Ikebana adds a touch of elegance to traditional temple festivals, honoring cultural traditions and spiritual connections.

K. **Moon Viewing (Tsukimi):** Ikebana arrangements are displayed during moon-viewing gatherings, enhancing the atmosphere of appreciation for the moon's beauty.

L. **Harvest Festivals (Niinamesai):** Ikebana decorations are used to celebrate the harvest, expressing gratitude for nature's bounty and abundance.

Seasonal Awareness

Japan's keen appreciation for the changing seasons can be tied to Ikebana, which has served as a visual calendar for centuries. You don't need to look too far to find this connection; it is expressly seen in Japanese agricultural practices and rituals. In modern Japan, Ikebana's role in mirroring the seasons remains evident in the nation's festivals, culinary traditions, and even digital expressions.

A. **Spring:** In spring, Ikebana's gentle arrangements mirror Japan's anticipation of cherry blossoms, capturing the delicate renewal of life after winter's slumber. For example, Ikebana enriches Hanami, a festival that takes place in Spring, with its delicate arrangements, embodying the essence of cherry blossoms and Japan's love for fleeting spring beauty.

B. **Summer:** As summer arrives, Ikebana's vibrant compositions reflect the energy of Japan's lively festivals and the lush growth that defines the season. During Gion Matsuri, an annual festival in Kyoto that celebrates the Yasaka Shrine, the adorning streets and shrines with colors are influenced by the art of Ikebana.

- **C. Autumn:** Ikebana embodies autumn's changing hues, gracefully mirroring Japan's reverence for the subtle shift from vibrant green to warm, golden tones. Tsukimi, the Japanese moon-viewing festival, embraces Ikebana, which reflects the moon's tranquility and Japan's reverence for autumn's peaceful allure.
- **D. Winter:** During winter's stillness, Ikebana stands as a reminder of Japan's appreciation for the beauty in simplicity, mirroring the tranquil landscapes of the season. For example, Ikebana's elegance offers warmth at the Sapporo Snow Festival, symbolizing beauty amidst winter's chill.

Continuation of Heritage

Ikebana's transmission from one generation to another aligns with Japan's emphasis on the preservation of cultural heritage. As the Ikenobo School evolved from the Meiji period to the present day, it encapsulated Japan's commitment to passing down traditional knowledge.

Ikebana has played a significant role in preserving Japan's cultural heritage by:

- A. Connecting People to Nature: Ikebana continues to emphemphasize mony between humans and nature, a core aspect of Japanese cultural identity.
- B. Transmitting Traditions: Ikebana has been practiced for centuries and is passed down through generations, contributing to the continuity of Japanese cultural heritage.
- C. Symbolism: Ikebana arrangements often incorporate symbolic elements, such as seasonal flowers and specific colors, which are deeply rooted in Japanese culture and traditions.
- D. Ceremonial and Ritual Use: Ikebana is used in various traditional ceremonies and rituals, like tea ceremonies and Shinto rituals, helping to maintain and showcase cultural practices.
- E. Artistic Expression: By practicing Ikebana, artisans express their creativity while adhering to traditional techniques and aesthetics, balancing innovation with tradition.
- F. Architectural Influence: Ikebana has influenced Japanese architecture and interior design, fostering a sense of cultural continuity in modern spaces.
- G. Educational Value: Ikebana schools offer lessons on

aesthetics, philosophy, and cultural values, educating students about Japanese heritage beyond just flower arranging.
H. **Global Recognition**: As Ikebana gains international popularity, it becomes a vehicle for sharing Japanese culture and fostering cross-cultural understanding.

Cross-Cultural Connection

Historical figures like Ellen Gordon Allen facilitated the introduction beyond Japan's shores. This art form has helped to preserve Japan's cross-cultural connections in the following ways:

A. **Cultural Exchange Initiatives**: Japan's cultural diplomacy initiatives align with Ikebana's spirit, strengthening international relationships through this revered art form.
B. **Universal Communication**: Ikebana's visual allure communicates Japan's culture universally, acting as a bridge that transcends language barriers.
C. **Tradition and Modernity Blend**: Ikebana's balance of tradition and innovation mirrors Japan's ability to harmonize its cultural legacy with contemporary trends.
D. **Soft Power Diplomacy**: Ikebana stands as a prime example of Japan's cultural soft power, fostering goodwill and dialogue on international platforms.
E. **Cultural Appreciation**: Sharing Ikebana with non-Japanese audiences preserves and shares Japan's unique aesthetics, contributing to the preservation of cultural heritage.

Education and Social Bonding

Ikebana classes foster more than just creative skills; they cultivate friendships and social connections. Community-building, connections among individuals of diverse backgrounds is possible today in Japan thanks in large part to Ikebana.

A. **Ikebana Schools during Edo Period**: Ikebana schools like Ikenobō were established during the Edo period, not only teaching floral arrangement but also nurturing social connections among students, contributing to a sense of community and shared culture.
B. **Ikebana Workshops in Contemporary Japan**: Modern Ikebana workshops continue to emphasize not just floral artistry, but also provide a space for individuals to

come together, forge friendships, and appreciate Japanese aesthetics.

C. **Community Ikebana Exhibitions**: Regular Ikebana exhibitions in local communities across Japan not only showcase artistic talent but also bring people from different walks of life together, fostering a sense of unity and cultural pride.

D. **Ikebana Classes in Urban Centers**: In bustling Japanese cities, Ikebana classes serve as places for people to unwind, learn a traditional skill, and interact with others, reinforcing social connections in a fast-paced modern society.

E. **Corporate Ikebana Workshops**: Many Japanese companies offer Ikebana workshops as team-building activities, allowing employees to collaborate creatively outside of their usual work tasks and strengthen workplace relationships.

F. **Ikebana Clubs in Universities**: Various universities in Japan have Ikebana clubs where students engage in artistic expression and build friendships, creating a sense of belonging and cultural appreciation among peers.

G. **Ikebana Social Media Communities**: Online platforms such as social media groups and forums dedicated to Ikebana enthusiasts provide an avenue for people across Japan to connect, share ideas, and form virtual friendships centered around their common interest.

Cultural Symbolism

Ikebana's careful selection of flowers and arrangements conveys Japan's cultural values and virtues. Throughout history, Ikebana has played a role in transmitting cultural messages through the following:

A. **Zen Buddhism**: During the Muromachi period, Zen Buddhism heavily influenced Ikebana, emphasizing minimalism and the appreciation of imperfection, reflecting Japan's reverence for nature and simplicity.

B. **Iemoto System and Hierarchy**: The traditional iemoto system, which designates a headmaster, embodies Japan's respect for tradition and hierarchical values, as students learn not just the art but also discipline and respect.

C. **Celebratory Ikebana Designs**: Ikebana is used in various celebrations and ceremonies, such as weddings and festivals, symbolizing unity, auspiciousness, and the continuation of cultural practices.

D. **Cultural Diplomacy**: Japan's government and organizations use Ikebana as a cultural ambassador, sharing its aesthetic and philosophical values with the world, fostering international understanding and appreciation.

E. **Incorporation in Modern Art**: Some contemporary artists incorporate Ikebana into their works, bridging traditional symbolism with modern expressions and echoing Japan's ability to blend heritage with innovation.

Healing and Well-being

Ikebana's meditative practice aligns with Japan's emphasis on holistic well-being. As practitioners arrange flowers with care, they find respite from the modern world's demands. In 21st century Japan, Ikebana's therapeutic qualities have prompted its inclusion in wellness programs, acknowledging its contribution to mental and emotional health.

A. **Ikebana Meditation Retreats**: These programs combine Ikebana practices with mindfulness and meditation techniques and offer participants a tranquil space to connect with nature and find inner peace.

B. **Corporate Stress Relief Workshops**: Japanese companies offer Ikebana workshops to employees as a way to manage workplace stress and encourage relaxation, allowing participants to unwind and recharge.

C. **Elderly Care Centers**: Ikebana sessions are conducted in elderly care facilities, providing seniors with a therapeutic outlet for creative expression and a sense of accomplishment, enhancing their overall well-being.

D. **Holistic Wellness Resorts**: Some wellness resorts in Japan incorporate Ikebana sessions into their programs, allowing guests to engage in mindful flower arranging as part of their rejuvenation experience.

E. **Wellness Retreats for Mental Health**: Modern wellness retreats in Japan focus on mental health and emotional well-being, integrating Ikebana to help participants connect with their emotions and find solace in the art form.

F. **Community Centers and Classes**: Local community centers offer Ikebana classes as a way for residents to engage in a soothing and artistic practice, fostering a sense of belonging and promoting mental wellness.

G. **Ikebana and Yoga Fusion**: Some wellness studios combine Ikebana workshops with yoga classes, creating a harmonious blend of movement, creativity, and relaxation for a holistic wellness experience.

Public Exhibitions

The Japanese government recognizes Ikebana's contribution to the nation's prosperity on a global scale. As a result, government support for Ikebana exhibitions have continued to heighten through the following:

A. **National Cultural Festivals**: Ikebana exhibitions are often featured as key attractions in Japan's national cultural festivals, showcasing the country's artistic heritage and attracting international visitors.

B. **Tourism Promotion**: Japan's tourism initiatives frequently highlight Ikebana exhibitions and this has helped to enhance the nation's reputation as a destination for art enthusiasts.

C. **Educational Partnerships**: Ikebana exhibitions cultivate an appreciation for cultural diversity and artistic expression by collaborating with educational institutions to expose students to traditional arts.

D. **Diplomatic Events**: Ikebana exhibitions are often featured at diplomatic events hosted by Japan and showcases the nation's creativity and cultural richness to international dignitaries.

Inspiration for Other Arts

Ikebana's cross-disciplinary inspiration echoes Japan's multifaceted creativity and its influence extends beyond floral arrangements, inspiring diverse artistic expressions, from literature to contemporary art forms.

Here are 12 examples of how Ikebana serves as inspiration for various arts in Japan:

A. **Literature**: Ikebana inspires Japanese poets to craft verses capturing nature's fleeting beauty.

B. **Painting**: Ikebana's balance guides painters, echoing Japan's aesthetic sensibilities.

C. **Ceramics**: Ikebana shapes pottery, resonating with Japan's reverence for functional beauty.

D. **Calligraphy**: Ikebana's lines influence calligraphy, mirroring Japan's artistic precision.

E. **Fashion Design**: Ikebana inspires fashion, reflecting Japan's blend of tradition and modernity.

F. **Interior Design**: Ikebana guides spaces, mirroring Japan's harmonious living environments.

G. **Performing Art**: Ikebana's calm echoes in Japan's graceful performing arts.

H. **Photography**: Ikebana's artistry inspires photographers, reflecting Japan's attention to detail.

I. **Cinematics**: Ikebana subtly enriches films, resonating with Japan's layered storytelling.

J. **Contemporary Art**: Ikebana's fusion of old and new influences modern Japanese art.

K. **Music and Composition**: Ikebana guides music composition, mirroring Japan's harmonic melodies.

L. **Digital Art**: Ikebana's aesthetics inspire digital artists, echoing Japan's visual sophistication.

CHAPTER 8: BONUS CHAPTER

DIY IKEBANA - MY PERSONAL IKEBANA TIPS TO YOU

My journey to becoming the Ikebana artist I am today has been eventful, to say the least. I have made mistakes and masterpieces, I have learned and grown. I won't say it's been the smoothest of rides, but I'll definitely say that I have no regrets whatsoever. The joy of seeing my creative ideas come to life is second to none and I would not trade it for anything.

In this bonus chapter, I share with you my most personal Ikebana tips to help you become the best Ikebana artist you could possibly be. I'll take you through some of the mistakes I made, the lessons learned, and the dos and don'ts of Ikebana that will elevate your game.

Without further ado, let's jump right in.

MISTAKES AND LESSONS

I will begin with mistakes because I have come to realize that, oftentimes, people see Ikebana experts as impeccable. But the truth is we are not (at least, I can say that for myself).

As a matter of fact, one of the things responsible for who I am today are the mistakes I have made and the many lessons that came with them. So, dear artist, it's important to remember that the path to becoming an Ikebana artist is not without its hiccups. Don't be afraid to make mistakes but more importantly, ensure to take the lessons that accompany your frailties.

I vividly recall a time when I was overzealous with my stem placement, resulting in a cluttered and chaotic arrangement. My Ikebana was so off-point, you would think my creation was inspired by a thick forest.

I had haphazardly arranged my flowers in such a way that there was no space. Not one! In my head at the time, it made no sense to create empty spaces.

My initial disappointment turned into a valuable lesson. With practice and reflection, I learned the art of restraint – the beauty of letting each stem breathe and making intentional choices that amplify the arrangement's beauty. I paid more attention to negative spaces and embraced the concept of *Ma*. These lessons elevated my Ikebana to a whole different level.

Similarly, there were instances when my arrangements didn't quite capture the emotion I intended. In those moments, I discovered the importance of patience and the willingness to iterate. Each mistake became a stepping stone towards mastering the art of Ikebana. Through trial and error, I unearthed a reservoir of creativity and learned to listen to my instincts.

Mistake made + lesson learned = Genius creation. Don't forget this!

PRACTICE MAKES PERFECTION

As you navigate the world of DIY Ikebana, remember that practice is your greatest ally. Just like pianists hone their skills through hours of playing, you'll find your Ikebana skills improving with each arrangement you create. Every snip of the scissors, every stem you place, is an opportunity to refine your artistry.

Ikebana is a journey, not a destination. Embrace imperfections and view them as badges of progress. Always bear in mind that with each arrangement, you're not just creating beauty; you're creating memories and stories that reflect your growth. Through practice, you'll gain the confidence to experiment, to innovate, and to let your unique voice shine through your arrangements.

DOs and DON'Ts OF IKEBANA

You will only make progress as an Ikebana artist when you learn the dos and don'ts of the craft. In this section, I have highlighted the rules to follow to help you achieve success in your art.

Allow these dos and don'ts to become not just guidelines, but also reflections of the emotions and experiences that make Ikebana a transformative art form.

Dos of Ikebana

1) Embrace Imperfections

Every time I allowed a slightly crooked stem to find its place in an arrangement, I felt a sense of liberation. Imperfections aren't flaws; they're the abstract elements that give your Ikebana creation depth and character.

In my early days of Ikebana, I often obsessed over achieving perfectly symmetrical arrangements. But as I gained more experience, I realized that nature's beauty isn't symmetrical – it's wonderfully imperfect. For instance, I discovered that the beauty of a slightly tilted stem or an asymmetrical balance is that it captures the essence of nature's whimsy.

Embracing imperfections not only adds uniqueness to your arrangement but also reflects the authenticity of your creative journey.

I also recall the exhilaration of trying unconventional combinations – pairing delicate blooms with rugged branches, or contrasting bold colors with subtle hues. Little did I know that each experiment was a step towards discovering my own Ikebana identity.

One memorable experiment involved integrating unexpected elements from my garden into my arrangement. I plucked a few sprigs of wild grass and intertwined them with vibrant blooms. The result was a harmonious blend of wildness and elegance that made the arrangement truly special.

Embracing experimentation allowed me to break free from convention and create arrangements that spoke to my heart's desires.

2) Maintain Hygiene

The act of cleaning my tools and vases is more than just a chore; it's a gesture of respect for the flowers that will grace them. To me, the routine of maintaining hygiene is a ritual of gratitude to the beauty that nature offers.

Early on in my journey, I made a nasty habit of keeping my tools clean and my vases unkempt. I would leave them so full of residue because I thought emptying the residue after using my vases never mattered. The consequences were evident – my blooms were wiltering so fast, and my arrangement lacked the vitality it deserved.

Learning from this mistake, I established a habit of thorough cleaning after each use. This practice not only extends the lifespan of my arrangements but also deepens my connection to the art of Ikebana.

Sharpen and sterilize your pruning shears. Wash your water vessel and Kenzan, and keep your surrounding environment clean. Do your flowers and foliage this huge favor and you will be amazed at how grateful they will be to you.

Don'ts of Ikebana

1) Don't Overcomplicate

There's a sense of relief that comes with simplicity. Just as life finds balance in its uncomplicated moments, so does Ikebana. Therefore, you must learn to embrace the elegance of simplicity, and allow your blooms to shine in their unadorned beauty.

Early in my Ikebana journey, I had a tendency to overthink my arrangements. I would add more stems, more foliage, and more elements, hoping to create something extraordinary. However, these arrangements often felt cluttered and overwhelming.

Over time, I learned that simplicity can be more impactful. Allowing a few carefully selected stems to take center stage allows their individual beauty to shine, resulting in arrangements that evoke a sense of tranquility and appreciation.

2) Never Be in a Hurry

The art of Ikebana has taught me the beauty of patience. As I stand before my arrangement, I'm reminded to slow down, to appreciate the process, and to find joy in every deliberate movement.

During a particularly busy period of my life, I attempted to create an Ikebana arrangement hastily, hoping to squeeze it into my schedule. The result was far from satisfying – stems were placed hastily, and the arrangement lacked the harmony I typically aim for.

This experience was a gentle reminder that Ikebana is not meant to be rushed. Taking the time to carefully select each stem, to arrange them thoughtfully, and to pause and reflect imbues the arrangement with a sense of mindfulness and intention.

3) Don't Forget Water Changes

Each time I change the water in my Ikebana vase, it's not just a practical task; it's an act of renewal. I'm not just sustaining the blooms; I'm infusing them with life, reminding myself of the continuous cycle of growth and transformation.

There were instances when I neglected to change the water in my Ikebana arrangement, thinking it was a minor detail. However, this oversight resulted in blooms that wilted prematurely and lost their vibrancy. The lesson was clear – neglecting the essential task of changing the water disrupts the arrangement's vitality and robs it of its full potential.

Regular water changes not only extend the life of your blooms but also reflect your dedication to nurturing their beauty.

DIY IKEBANA ARRANGEMENT YOU CAN TRY OUT ON YOUR OWN

Let's take a step further by transforming these insights into hands-on creations that not only bring you joy but also allow you to express your unique voice through Ikebana. I have given each of these arrangements a name that I feel captures their essence:

Minimalist Elegance
My journey with minimalist Ikebana began with an arrangement of just a single branch and a single blossom. This simplicity was a revelation.

The absence of excess allowed each element to command attention, showcasing their inherent beauty. This arrangement taught me the art of restraint, of allowing nature's wonders to take center stage. It was a gentle reminder that less is often more – that simplicity can speak volumes and captivate hearts.

You can achieve minimalism in your Ikebana by selecting a single stem that captivates you and placing it in a tall, elegant vase. Let it stand alone, radiating its presence and inviting admiration.

Serenity in a Bowl
I often find solace in arranging blooms in a shallow bowl filled with water. The effect is always breathtaking – the water's surface cradles the petals, creating a scene that echoes the beauty of nature's waterways. This arrangement transports me to a world of serenity and reflection.

You too can try this by filling a shallow bowl with water and gently float a few blooms on its surface. The ripples that form around the blooms will add a dynamic touch, while the reflection in the water will create a sense of depth. This arrangement is a poetic reminder to embrace life's quiet moments, to find beauty in stillness, and to let your creativity flow like water.

Vibrant Verticality

One of my favorite Ikebana memories revolves around creating a vertical arrangement that incorporated stems of varying lengths. As I added each stem, the arrangement seemed to come alive, exuding energy and positivity. Personally, this design was a testament to the power of upward movement, of striving towards one's goals with determination and zest.

How do you go about this? Simply select an assortment of blooms in different colors and sizes. Begin by placing the tallest stem at the center of the vase and gradually add shorter stems around it. As you work your way down, the arrangement will take on a dynamic, ascending form.

Nature's Harmony

One of my most memorable Ikebana experiences was crafting an arrangement that paid homage to nature's colors. I gathered stems of various shades of green, from deep emerald to delicate mint. As I placed each stem in a cascading formation, the arrangement transformed into a visual representation of nature's balance and unity.

You can also attempt this arrangement by collecting stems in shades of green that remind you of a tranquil forest. Again, begin by placing the tallest stem at the center of the vase and let the others cascade around it.

Blossoms in the Wind

One of my Ikebana experiments involved arranging blooms in a way that simulated the fluidity of wind-blown petals. I chose delicate flowers with slender stems and allowed them to arch and curve, evoking a sense of motion. The result was an arrangement that seemed to capture a moment frozen in time.

Try this arrangement by selecting blooms with slender stems and delicate petals. Arrange them in a way that mimics the movement of wind-blown petals. Allow the stems to curve and sway, creating a sense of graceful motion.

CONCLUSION

Final Thoughts and Next Steps

In bidding adieu to this immersive exploration of Ikebana, let your heart swell with the realization that you, my cherished reader, have embarked upon a journey of profound resonance. As we stand at the confluence of parting thoughts and the path that beckons ahead, let the radiant petals of your newfound understanding unfurl, bathing you in the warm embrace of nature's artistry and your own creative spirit.

This odyssey through Ikebana's world has not been mere instruction; it has been an invitation to commune with nature, to dance with petals and leaves, and to compose symphonies of emotions through your artistic touch. Your heart has connected with the heartbeats of flowers, and in each arrangement, you've etched your aspirations, your joys, and your dreams onto the canvas of existence.

What lies ahead is more than a mere conclusion; it's an overture to a symphony of self-discovery, a prelude to the crescendo of creative expression. This isn't the end; it's the beginning of your journey as an Ikebana artist, a storyteller whose medium is the language of petals, stems, and form.

As you bid farewell to these pages, know that you're not alone. The emotions stirred within you, the connections forged with nature, and the stories told through your arrangements bind you to a lineage of Ikebana practitioners spanning centuries. Every time you touch a stem or breathe life into a composition, you echo the whispers of countless artists who came before you.

Ikebana isn't just about arranging flowers; it's about arranging emotions. With each arrangement, you're scribing your narrative, your innermost feelings, and your unique perspective onto the canvas of existence. These compositions resonate with an authenticity that is uniquely yours—a symphony that reverberates with the harmonious rhythm of your soul.

Let the weight of these words linger, dear reader, as you embark on this journey of Ikebana. As you carefully place each stem, remember that your arrangements breathe with the sincerity of your emotions. Your heart's cadence is woven into every curve and bend, every twist and turn.

Embrace Ikebana as more than an art form; embrace it as a mirror reflecting the cultural tapestry of Japan. As you thread the philosophy of Ikebana through your practice, you're harmonizing your journey with this age-old wisdom. The arrangements you delicately craft, akin to fleeting moments suspended in the tendrils of time, possess the unique power to encapsulate the very essence of life's transient journey. As you take that step into the enchanting world of Ikebana, you're not merely crafting art; you're embodying a profound homage to a philosophy that resonates deeply, enriching your connection with nature's ephemeral beauty.

Dear reader, I implore you to embrace this philosophy with open arms as you set forth upon your personal odyssey. As you navigate the intricate path of this art form, let it become your sanctuary—a space where the petals and leaves you manipulate form the foundation of your expressive tapestry. Amidst the ebb and flow of creation, remember that each vessel, each element you touch, is a canvas yearning for the brushstrokes of your unique artistic voice.

Don't be daunted by the blank vase before you; it's a canvas yearning for your emotions to unfold upon it. Take the tools, the techniques, and the inspiration garnered from these pages, and embark on your Ikebana journey with confidence and curiosity.

You need not fear any missteps, for each "mistake" is but a brushstroke on your canvas of growth. Mistakes, after all, are the stepping stones to mastery. Let the emotions unfurl, let the creativity soar, and let Ikebana become a channel for you to express the depths of your soul. You stand on the precipice of an artistic odyssey—one that is boundless, enchanting, and uniquely your own.

So, as you bid adieu to these pages, remember that the story doesn't end here; it evolves with every arrangement you conceive. Let your petals be your voice, your leaves be your language, and your arrangements be the testament to your beautiful journey. Embrace your emotions, dear reader, embrace the canvas of existence, and embrace Ikebana as the wondrous medium that connects you to the heartbeat of the universe. Your journey has begun; may your petals forever bloom in the garden of creativity.

Printed in Dunstable, United Kingdom